CW00701850

ROCK VALLEY AN
LANE RECOLL˷ ΙΙΟΝS

A HISTORY OF BARRINGER WALLIS AND
MANNERS AND THE MANSFIELD AND
SUTTON-IN-ASHFIELD BRANCHES OF THE
METAL BOX COMPANY

Alan Atkins

(Edited and Compiled by Alan Plowright)

Moorfield Press

Published in Great Britain
by
Moorfield Press 2006

Page Layout by
Highlight Type Bureau Ltd. Bradford, West Yorkshire
Printed in England by
The Amadeus Press, Cleckheaton, West Yorkshire

A CIP catalogue record for this book is available from the
British Library

ISBN O 9530 11976

Cover Photograph (front) - Sketch of Rock Valley Works, 1914
Cover Photograph (back) - Sketch of Oddicroft Lane Works, 1914

Contents

Acknowledgements

I would like to pay tribute all those who have freely passed on their knowledge, or contributed in any way towards the compilation of this book. My special thanks are extended to the following:

Mr J.E.Walsh, whose assistance has been invaluable.

Mr C.I.Mellor for his vital contribution of the diary of events relating to the commercial aspects of tin-box manufacture and for his recent additional notes.

Mrs. Nora Beckett who brought to life the early office working arrangements and related memories of her many friends.

Brian Hall, Gordon Beastall and Keith Pearcy for the account of the disastrous fire at the Sutton-in-Ashfield Factory.

Miss Eva Shaw, Mrs. Rose Draycott, Miss Jean Teare and Arthur Littlewood (Junior) for their contribution to the history of the early years.

Joan Abbott (Bull) for information regarding employees at Sutton-in-Ashfield.

Andy Kaye, Manager of the Rock Valley Factory, now operating as Crown Speciality Packaging, for his valuable assistance.

The Old Mansfield Society.

Jeremy Plews, Editor of the 'Chad,' for supplying helpful archive material.

Those too numerous to mention whose assistance in obtaining documentation and checking data is greatly appreciated.

Foreword

One of the many friends I had the privilege of making, at the Mansfield branch of the Metal Box Company, prompted me to compile this memoir. He was Charles Fletcher, a commercial design artist who passed away at the grand old age of 103. It is also through such inspirational friendships that I received much of the material used in this book. Although some of its content concerns the development and processes of the two companies, it is the employees that formed their life-blood. My most vivid memories are of the 'characters' who passed through over the years and 'oiled the wheels' of our daily endeavours, leaving an indelible imprint on all who met them.

Thanks are given, in the 'Acknowledgements' section, to the people who have kindly contributed to this publication, but may I also pay tribute to the many friends and colleagues that made my time at 'Metal Box' so unforgettable.

I trust that the following pages will make interesting reading, particularly from the local history standpoint. I feel that the recording of the period from 1895 to 1983 is vitally important because the names of Barringer Wallis and Manners and the Metal Box Company should always be remembered for their excellence in tin-box manufacture and the employment of a dedicated and accomplished workforce. One hopes that this sector of the packaging industry maintains its fine traditions and continues to flourish.

Alan Atkins 2006

Introduction

This history, in its various forms, is the result of four years research, which revealed several manuscripts that had not been combined into one document. The process of compilation was begun by TWW (Tom) Peacock and it has proved to be a vital historical record of the tin box and canister industry in Mansfield and Sutton-in-Ashfield.

A paper, compiled by C.I. Mellor in 1965, has added an indispensable insight into the commercial aspects of the business. In addition, an article by J. E. Walsh, which relates his experiences over many years spent at the Mansfield branch of the Metal Box Company, provides a unique record from the viewpoint of a long-serving member of management.

The story begins in 1839 when David Cooper Barringer obtained a transfer of the lease for a Mustard Mill in Rock Valley, Mansfield. From these small beginnings the business began to grow when the idea of packing mustard in fancy tins was conceived. A tin-making plant was installed in 1884 and, in 1893, printing directly onto tinplate was introduced. Two years later the firm evolved into the Limited Company, Barringer Wallis and Manners.

In 1897 space was at a premium and, with little room to expand in Rock Valley, a Cotton-Doubling Mill was purchased, together with ten acres of surrounding land, at Oddicroft Lane, Sutton-in-Ashfield, for £2,800. During the nineteenth century the mill had belonged to the Adlington family who became joined by marriage to the Stokes family that had foundry and engineering interests, including Stokes Castings. Various extensions were made to the premises over the following years and the toy section of the business was eventually concentrated there between the wars.

Just before the outbreak of war, in 1939, the firm was

taken over by the Metal Box Company, who had numerous branches nationwide. At the end of the Second World War, new management, machinery and production methods were introduced. Control systems were being standardised throughout the company and these, together with skilled and well-trained personnel, ensured a reputation for excellence.

In addition to the mainstay of the business, known as 'General Line' production (i.e. decorated tin boxes, trays and toys), the manufacture of open top cans was commenced in 1947. Extruded aluminium containers were in their infancy at this time, but their production would eventually become a vital part of the enterprise. The Extrusion Department began in the 1930s producing collapsible tubes made from tinplate (i.e. 'Gibbs Dentifrice'). Unfortunately, the Second World War intervened before the production of aluminium tubes was commenced.

Products were supplied to countless companies, both nationally and worldwide. The foundations had been laid for the prosperity and well-being of the Mansfield and Sutton branches of the Metal Box Company until 1983, the year that this historical insight terminates.

William Holmes Reddan
Managing Director of Barringer Wallis and Manners
from 1905 to 1923

CHAPTER ONE

The Folk of Rock Valley and Oddicroft Lane

1895 to 1924

We begin our look at the people who were employed at Barringer Wallis and Manners and the Mansfield and Sutton branches of the Metal Box Company, in 1895, when the former came into being as a limited company. At this time Robert Barringer, who became the proprietor of the mustard business at Rock Valley in 1861 had been retired for six years. Although he was never connected with the new company its existence was, in a large part, due to him.

Despite Robert's advancing age he was well respected in the town and became its mayor in 1896, having served conscientiously on the Mansfield Borough Council for five years, as a Liberal. That year was an eventful one for him. He organised the celebrations and decoration of the town in recognition of Queen Victoria's Diamond Jubilee. In addition he received the Prince and Princess of Wales when they visited Mansfield accompanied by the Duke and Duchess of Portland. In 1897 he attended Queen Victoria's reception at Buckingham Palace, where he was required to wear formal Court Dress, including knee breeches and sword. Later that year Robert was invited to visit the Queen at Windsor Castle.

Robert was a lifelong member of the Society of Friends, was made an Alderman and became chairman of the Waterworks Committee when the Waterworks Company was bought out. In this capacity he became involved on a daily basis with the Rainworth Water Scheme, so much so that one of the pumping engines was named 'Barringer.' Robert died in 1905 and, like a number of his Quaker friends he was interred in the graveyard of the Friends Meeting House, Mansfield.

The first directors of Barringer Wallis and Manners were Walter Barringer, Isaac Wallis and Charles Manners. The latter was appointed Managing Director and the company had an office in Fleet Street, London, which had been the business address of Charles' father, George Manners.

In 1907 Isaac Wallis, aged 52, was elected Mayor of Mansfield and was also appointed a Justice of the Peace. The brother-in-law of Robert Barringer, he came to Mansfield in 1879 to join the tin-box branch of the business. Like Robert he was a Liberal and a reformist. He was a very popular public speaker and was elected to Mansfield Borough Council in 1894, serving as a councillor for seventeen years.

Isaac was a keen sportsman who enjoyed rugby football and cricket, being an accomplished amateur batsman. He encouraged the factory employees to participate in football, cricket and tennis. Trophies, donated by the directors, were competed for on an inter-factory basis with employees from other local companies

His special interest was education, both elementary and secondary and he also supported the Adult School Movement, which met at the Friends Meeting House. It is largely due to his efforts that a gift from Andrew Carnegie of £1000 enabled the public library to be built on Leeming Street. Isaac was also instrumental in a library being opened in Pleasley Hill after a special appeal to Mrs. Carnegie.

A love of poetry resulted in his publication of two volumes of such, in 1905 and 1928. In 1924 he published the biography of one of the Headmasters of Ackworth School, Yorkshire, which he attended as a boy. He also supported the work of the R.S.P.C.A. and frequently opened the grounds of his home on Crow Hill Drive for that and other worthy causes.

Robert Barringer's resilience and youthful outlook shortly before his retirement from the firm was a revelation to Isaac. He recalls Robert being an early riser and his joining him and his son, Walter Barringer, frequently for coffee at the coffee tavern in Westgate at 6am.

Isaac's day to day involvement in Barringer Wallis and Manners was said to be financial and his good business brain made him a 'back room wizard.' It is no surprise that he eventually became chairman of the company. He died in 1933, aged 78 and, unusually for those times, he was cremated and his ashes were interred in the graveyard of the Friends Meeting House.

Charles Manners was a great asset to the company having set about building up the concern in 1891. His business and financial ability were exceptional and he was also a good organiser and an experienced salesman. His main contributions to the firm, in the view of Isaac Wallis, were his daring and spacious outlook, his courage and his skill in providing the necessary finances for new equipment. Charles provided the stimulant of a more adventurous outlook to his fellow directors and the success of the firm in its early years was greatly due to his unfailing optimism and enthusiasm.

In addition to his business career Charles had a creative social obligation, which resulted in his involvement in many of the activities of the town. He was a prominent Freemason, a member of the Hospital Board and a committee member of the Mechanics Institute, Mansfield Tennis Club and Mansfield Golf Club.

His work on behalf of the Mansfield School of Art deserves particular recognition. Eager to make improvements, Charles was instrumental in the transfer of the school from the Mechanics Institute to Commercial Street and in the securing of a grant to furnish the new premises.

Charles was probably best known for his kindness, comradeship and helpfulness. The following anecdote illustrates the helpful interest he took in his friends and his prompt manner of dealing with their difficulties.

Late one evening, a visitor was announced, who proved to be an old school friend, somewhat down on his luck. The man was an agent for a firm that dealt in washing machines, which, it was explained, were modelled on the cradles used for gold washing in the American and Colonial gold fields. Charles insisted that the machine was demonstrated immediately and it was promptly set up in the drawing room. Realising the possible dangers, the machine was moved to the scullery where it received a very cold reception from the maid who strongly disapproved of her spotless premises being turned into a washroom at so late an hour. However, the machine was set in motion and the salesman, perspiring freely, endeavoured to prove that the dirt had disappeared from the garments within. Unfortunately it did not, but it was an improvement on the dolly tub and a good number of machines were sold in the district, thanks to Charles' good nature.

An early type of motor car (the eight horsepower De Dion) aroused his enthusiasm and his adventures in the vehicle were numerous. He realised that motor transport was the thing of the future and he and several friends initiated a motorbus service. After a hair-raising journey from the South, they brought the 'Pioneer' to Mansfield. The scheme was not a great success as the vehicle was apt to lose its tyres and was unreliable, but it proved to be a harbinger of things to come.

1905 saw the untimely death of Charles Manners. On June 23rd Isaac Wallis was surprised to hear that Charles had been taken ill with a bad attack of sciatica, probably due to a drenching whilst motoring to Nottingham. Pneumonia soon set in and Charles died three days later. It was a great loss to the firm and the town.

Another person to contribute towards the early success of Barringer Wallis and Manners was William Holmes Reddan who joined the firm in 1896. He was the son of the manager of the Mustard Mill. His wide knowledge and experience in the printing trade, combined with a fine sense of organisation and leadership, were quickly recognised and, within a short period of time, he was elected to the Board of Directors. When Charles Manners died suddenly in 1905, William Holmes Reddan took over as Managing Director, a position he occupied until his death in 1923.

Walter Barringer joined the company from school and he devoted all his time and energy to it. From the outset his interest in the business was absorbing and he was methodical and conscientious in all his dealings. He began by working in every department of the mill and learned the business thoroughly, which put him in good stead when he became a member of the management.

During the latter half of the 1870's and through most of the 1880's Walter was usually at work by 6am and, in the busy months was working until 9pm. However, it must be said that similar hours were observed by the workforce at that time.

An excellent judge of mustard seed, he knew instinctively when a sample would yield well and, through his acute sense of smell, he could detect immediately if seed was out of condition. Walter's presence made it possible for William Holmes Reddan, who was an accomplished salesman, to devote his time to the sales side of the operation. The Midland and Eastern Counties were covered methodically and efficiently, providing a sound base for progress. Several Sales Representatives were recruited during those years. The first of these, W.H. Frew, joined the company in 1898 and covered the Glasgow area. Then came H.G.W.Claringbull, in 1900, whose extensive 'patch' was designated the 'Midlands,' although it covered an area stretching from Lancashire down to Bristol and even encompassed Ireland. Amongst his earliest customers were Ogdens and Hignetts of Liverpool, Wills of Bristol, Gallaghers of Belfast and Davies of Chester. All these companies purchased tobacco containers and tablets.

The remainder of the sales force comprised D.P.Bedford, who arrived in 1901 and J.W.D. Simmons, recruited in 1905.

James Kirkbride had joined the business in 1893, from Hudson Scott of Carlisle, a firm owned by a Quaker family and in direct competition with Barringer Wallis and Manners. Hudson Scott had the slight edge as regards the printing side of the business and James was brought in to oversee a new printing process, that of transfer printing, followed later by offset printing.

James, who was greatly respected, was promoted to Factory Manager. The perfect gentleman, he toured the works each morning dressed in typical Edwardian style, complete with bowler hat, black tie and waistcoat with gold watch and chain. One of the production lines that attracted him was employed on soldering and, because it was a quiet part of the factory the girls could often be heard singing as they worked. One day James told them he did not mind their singing, provided it was hymns that they sang.

A keen follower of football, he often accompanied the Barringer Wallis and Manners football team to local league matches. There is a photograph in existence of James at such a match in 1916.

Another Victorian/Edwardian character was Charles Harris, a very tall man, who lived in the vicinity of the factory, on Woodhouse Road. Like James Kirkbride he was always well-dressed, normally sporting a dark suit and starched shirt and collar. He was in charge of the busy Despatch Department, which, at that time, encompassed many operations. An ex-soldier belonging to a Cavalry Regiment, (possibly the Sherwood Rangers) he had a typical military bearing and appearance - back straight as a ramrod, trousers immaculately creased, and shoes shining like mirrors. These features were topped with neatly combed sparse hair and, in his later years, a magnificent white moustache.

His department was adjacent to the I.B.U. (Irregular Built Up) area, which became overloaded. Some presses were sited in the Despatch Department for the manufacture of certain items in the 'stock box' business, illustrated in a handsome ('Seasons') catalogue, which incorporated a range of tea caddies and confectionery tins. The department also performed the filling of some of these containers, (for issue to the customers' commercial travellers) with biscuits and sweets. To facilitate this, customers often supplied consignments of biscuits and sweets and, on one occasion when some biscuits were required for packing into tins the biscuits supplied by the customer had miraculously disappeared!

Arthur Taylor came to the Mustard Mill in 1891 immediately after leaving Daniel Maltby's school, which was situated close to Rock Valley. His home was in Warsop and he walked the three or four miles to work each morning always arriving at the Mustard Mill by six a.m. His first duty was attending to a tin box kept inside the office window. The workers pushed their time checks through a slot in the window and into this receptacle. At six fifteen a.m. the box was removed.

For three or four years Arthur acted as office boy and letter-copying was one of his duties, both at the Mustard Mill and later at the Tin Works. Charles Manners had a typewriter, which he and Arthur used for correspondence, but as the workload increased a full-time typist, Miss King, was engaged and a replacement office boy was appointed.

As the years passed Arthur rose to become Company Secretary. He presided over his open office, christened the 'Counting House,' at a high desk from which he kept everyone under surveillance. Despite his being a strong disciplinarian he was a kind-hearted and benevolent person and everyone held him in high regard.

Mr Trethowan, who eventually became head of the Lithographic Artists' Department, joined the firm in 1891 and in his early days he shared a tiny room, accessed by a spiral staircase, with Mr Lamb and Mr Moses. The former was the first lettering artist and the latter the first lithographic artist and designer. Space was at a premium in the minute office, which was completely filled by its three occupants.

The inspirational Charles Fletcher began working for the company in 1906, aged fourteen. He was an apprentice artist, who would later become a commercial artist of international renown. A lifelong bachelor, he attended Mansfield College of Art, which, at that time was situated at the bottom of Chesterfield Road. In later life Charles frequently recalled the years of the First World War when the factory was committed to producing components for the war effort. These included mess tins, ammunition and shell cases, gas mask components and biscuit tins.

At that time of war, Charles recollected, the factory girls often brought their knitting to work, for many of them were knitting socks for the troops engaged in the French campaign. At meal times out would come the wool and knitting needles and the girls would knit furiously.

It should be remembered that many male employees were called to the colours and a considerable number did not return. William Holmes Reddan, on the occasion of the laying of the stone for the factory extension, in 1919, made a moving reference to their loss.

Charles Fletcher became a craftsman in his own right. At that time artists were employed by Barringer Wallis and Manners on a contract, or commission basis, but the designs, in many cases, were the copyright of the company. However, Charles will be most remembered for his design of the 'Quality Street' range of containers. He earned the nickname, 'Mr Quality Street' and his designs were so successful they are still with us today.

Soon after the First World War Charles became interested in travel, particularly on the railways. He lived in Bishop Street, Mansfield, that was very close to the London Midland and Scottish Railway station, in fact the station-master lived in a house at the bottom of the street. Charles nicknamed him 'Turnip' on account of his short stature and bald head. At that time a train left Mansfield station every four minutes, making it busier than St. Pancras! Charles had many tales to tell about this era of steam and his excursions by rail.

Very interested in music and the arts, Charles was also a good billiards and snooker player and he loved cricket. As a season ticket holder of Nottinghamshire County Cricket Club he spent much time at the Trent Bridge ground.

Cyril Mallatrat, an artist who specialised in Elizabethan, Edwardian, and Victorian designs, including portraits, was a rival to Charles. Both artists had their own studios in the Artists' Department, which reflected their seniority and they visited the Victoria and Albert Museum regularly and also other similar establishments both at home and abroad. These offered the opportunity to discover material for use in their designs.

Two other artists were commissioned during this period, namely G. Willis and T. H. Collins.

1924 to 1939

A good proportion of the management of Barringer Wallis and Manners, up until the time of the Second World War, were Quakers and it is interesting to note that so were most of the factory owners in the tin box industry in the North of

England.

In 1924 the board of Barringer Wallis and Manners consisted of the following :

Isaac Henry Wallis (Chairman)

Robert Manners, son of Charles Manners, (Joint Managing Director).

Gustave N.F. Reddan, son of William Holmes Reddan, (Joint Managing Director).

William G. Maltby (Commercial Director).

Robert Manners was brought from his scholastic surroundings to serve an engineering apprenticeship, which gave him a grasp of the technical side of production. At the same time Gustave Reddan was transferred from college in order to gain an insight into the world of commerce, before taking up his duties with the company. These two young men, together with their future colleague William Maltby, were thus able to accumulate a thorough knowledge of the business that they would one day control.

Robert became Technical Manager of the Mansfield and Sutton factories before his elevation to the board. He also became a director of Mansfield Standard Sand Company and sadly he died in 1944 at the age of fifty-six. He was remembered with great affection by all who knew him and admired for his contribution to the business and its employee's interests.

Charles Fletcher was always happy to relate a tale concerning Gustave Reddan, who, in his early days with the firm was responsible for customer designs and the progress of artwork. However, not fully understanding the elements of design and art preparation, Gustave thought it was possible to cut the time needed to reproduce a design (in this case from an exhibit in the Victoria and Albert Museum) being painted on a container for customer approval. The artist commissioned to prepare the design for the container was G. Willis and Gustave called on him in order to discuss the artwork. As he was leaving Gustave said, 'I will collect this work in four days,' to which Willis replied, 'Come back in fourteen days.' Gustave retorted, 'Willis, I am the boss and I want this work in four days.' Willis sprang to his feet and said, 'You maybe a boss, but my boss you will never be!' Immediately, Willis collected his case and left the premises.

On hearing the news of this confrontation William Holmes Reddan was furious with his son and ordered him to make his peace with Willis. At the time Willis was employed on another commission for a local printing company and, as it would take ten days to complete, Charles Fletcher was asked to mediate with him. Willis agreed to return when this commission was completed.

The above story highlights the independence of the artists at that time, who took a great pride in their work. Although a breed apart they normally showed significant loyalty to the company.

Gustave Reddan eventually became a respected member of the board. He encouraged sporting contests against other factories, notably at football, tennis and swimming. Local industry was encouraged to compete annually for the many awards and trophies that bore his name. One such firm was the Mansfield Shoe Company, which was owned at that time by the Royce family.

William G. Maltby was responsible for tinplate supplies and commercial dealings with major customers, such as Players and Boots of Nottingham. His office was often referred to as the 'Home Office.'

William was greatly interested in music and local history, as were Charles Manners and Isaac Wallis. The notable Barringer's Girls' Choir entertained audiences on many occasions in those days.

J. E. (Eddie) Walsh arrived at the Rock Valley Works one day in May 1933 to be interviewed for a post in the company's Transport Department. He was aged twenty-two and had been slightly overawed by the style and quality of the letter, which had summoned him for interview. Typed on high quality coloured paper, in light brown ink, its heading displayed a statement of the patronage bestowed on the company by the reigning King George V and Queen Mary. This regal atmosphere was further emphasised when Eddie was ushered into a room containing several wall hangings of heavy, mahogany-framed documents, which, on closer inspection, turned out to be Royal Warrants of Approval, granted to the company by a succession of monarchs. Later, this awestruck young man was to see a commemorative plaque of the visit by King George V and Queen Mary to the 'Tin Works,' as the factory was then known, which took place in 1914. Eddie also observed a visitor's book containing the signatures of their majesties and members of the royal party, together with the handsome silver ink stand and pen used for the signing.

Prior to the interview Eddie had, in his opinion, submitted adequate testimonials as to his education and his ability in the job he had held for six years after leaving school. However, his confidence was shaken when he was asked during the interview to complete a short test paper comprising English grammar, spelling and arithmetic. Later, he realised that the test was indicative of the meticulous way in which the company conducted their business. Happily, Eddie was successful in his application and he joined the company.

At that time, Eddie recalls, the operation of the business was divided between Gustave Reddan, (covering commercial and administration) and Robert Manners, who controlled production and technical affairs, including toolmaking and engineering. All commercial accounts, other than those dealt with by William Maltby, were handled by L.J.Wass (Commercial Manager), who was in charge of the Marketing (Commercial) Department. Nora Beckett records that the staff in those days consisted of herself, Miss Wright, Miss Smith and Freda Barrington, who eventually left the company. Freda married Jess Farmilo, who is referred to later in this account. Quotations were issued from this department to regular and potential customers and tinplate orders were originated. Works Orders were also issued and contacts were made with customers who often visited the factory. Nora Beckett (née Petitt) was transferred from the department to work for William Maltby until his retirement and, as referred to later, married Graham Beckett. Miss Gutteridge, sister to Ralph Gutteridge, was Gustave Reddan's private secretary.

A member of the field sales force of that period was J.D.Simmons, the son of J.W.D.Simmons who, as mentioned earlier, joined the company in 1905. Simmons Junior covered the Glasgow area and his fellow representatives were Mr Greenfield (Midland Area) and Mr Curtis (London Area), assisted by Mr Denman. They reported daily on their activities, which were summarised in a document entitled 'Extracts' that was circulated, by mid-morning, to all managers for the appropriate action.

Eddie Walsh also recalls many other work colleagues of the 1930's. One such person was Mr T. F. (Frank) Clarke who joined the company around 1910 and headed the Transport Department, which dealt with the transportation of the company's goods throughout the United Kingdom and overseas.

The Transport Department was also responsible for the distribution of metal toys to Burnett Ltd. It was handily placed next to the Toy Factory where their manufacture was carried out. Frank ran his department with the aid of four female assistants. A dour, but forceful man, he also displayed great patience, which colleagues attributed to his time as a prisoner of war during the 1914-1918 conflict.

To enlarge on the Transport Department, the garage was sited at the far end of Rock Valley and it was in the care of William Pallisser. He served as chief mechanic and chauffeur to Gustave Reddan and his unusual hobby was repairing sewing machines. Each director had a car at that time - Gustave Reddan, a Vauxhall, Robert Manners, a Railton and William Maltby, a Rover. In addition to these, an old Sunbeam served as a link between the Mansfield and Sutton-in-Ashfield factories. Amongst the commercial vehicles were an open-deck Leyland, often referred to as the 'Ten-tonner' and a smaller open Thorneycroft lorry. The Leyland was mainly used to convey boiler coal from Sherwood Colliery to the boiler house and tinplate, (which in those days was in boxes, not on pallets) from the railway stations to the tinplate stores. The transportation of light loads between the Mansfield and Sutton-in-Ashfield factories was carried out by the Thorneycroft, which also operated between the factories and the railway stations.

A well-remembered character was Harold Cooke who owned a horse, which he called 'Captain.' Harold was contracted to transport scrap tinplate from the factory to the railway sidings on Baums Lane, Mansfield, which at that time was the L.N.E.R. central goods depot. Alongside the depot were the engine sheds but the whole site was demolished some years ago and it is now occupied by the B&Q store. Harold's horse was so used to the route that all Harold was required to do was to shout, 'Gee up Captain!' when the wagon was fully loaded. The horse could then be seen leaving the factory and climbing out of Rock Valley with Harold ten yards or so behind, without a care in the world.

Harold owned a small farm on Littleworth, Mansfield, whose entrance was dominated by a large pear tree. This was a source of delight for the children attending nearby King Edward School who would share its fruit on the way home from school.

Arthur Littlewood (Senior), (followed later in the company by his son, also named Arthur) was in charge of the joiner's shop, which was adjacent to the garage. The Littlewood family lived in a stone cottage (now demolished) further up the yard and the River Maun ran virtually over the front doorstep.

Miss Agnes (Aggie) Betts rendered clerical assistance in the Despatch Department during this period, which was still under the watchful eye of the aforementioned Charles Harris. Although the department was sited in a dark subterranean cavern below what became the Press Shop, the area was lit by Aggie's sweet nature. A kind-hearted and diligent person, she always had a bag of sweets available, which she freely dispensed amongst her colleagues.

The overlooker/charge-hand was Edith Clark, a spinster and a very pleasant person. It is believed that the term 'overlooker' was used at that time because departmental offices were usually set on stilts in order that Edith and her counterparts could overlook the scene of operations. She was a staunch Methodist, who lived in Cavendish Street, Mansfield and each morning she walked to work with Nellie Merrill, who lived further down the street. Edith served the company faithfully until she retired at the age of sixty. Nellie, also a spinster and an ardent Methodist, was never heard to complain and seemed perfectly happy with her own company.

One of several people to transfer from Hudson Scott of Carlisle, was Frederick Edgar, who arrived in 1919. He was appointed Deputy Factory Manager and eventually became Factory Manager. The son of a Police Inspector, he lived in Shirburn Avenue, Mansfield, one hundred yards from the factory. Later, he moved to a bungalow near High Oakham School. He was a friend of my father Thomas Atkins, who had joined the company prior to the First World War. Frederick's wife, Winnie, was a wonderful person who regularly visited my parents once a week. Sadly, late in life, Frederick and Winnie were divorced and he left Mansfield to join Lines Bros. (Triang Toys) from which he retired a few years later.

Jack Horsfield followed Frederick from Hudson Scott in 1922. He was an engineer/toolmaker, who was in charge of the canister making up department, often referred to as Making II, or I.B.U. Jack lived on Forest Road, Mansfield and at first his accent was difficult to decipher, but he was a good engineer and superintendent. He was one of the few members of staff to own a car at that time, an Austin Seven. Jack married the forewoman of his department and they had a son, Alan, who later joined the printing staff of the company.

Another man to leave Hudson Scott to join Barringer Wallis and Manners was J. Armstrong, a printer by trade. He eventually took charge of the print shop at Mansfield and later at Sutton-in-Ashfield when it was moved there. In the years that followed many factory personnel transferred from what became the Carlisle branch of the Metal Box Company.

On the departure of Isaac Wallis, the Accounts Department was taken over by Arthur Lloyd Birks, a Quaker and a Borough Councillor, like his predecessor. He was a very able man who had joined the firm in 1929 as Factory Accountant, whose responsibilties included the Wages Department. A dominant, but honest and well-liked figure, Arthur retired around 1957 and was elected Mayor in 1960, following in the footsteps of his grandfather who was Mayor in 1897. In his Mayor making speech, Arthur had hoped to include news of a new Town Hall, but a visit from the County Planning Officer put a stop to that. On that occasion he said to Arthur, 'You must first let me plan a ring road for the town on which to put your Town Hall.'

For many years the Birks family were staunch members of the Unitarian Church at the Old Meeting House, in Mansfield and one of Arthur's ancestors had a beautiful stained glass window installed there. In later life Arthur attended the Parish Church of St Peter and St Paul and served on the Parish Council.

Another man destined to become Mayor of Mansfield (1957) was Alfred Arthur Armstrong who also joined the company in 1929. Born in Carlton in 1900 he settled in Newcastle before moving to Mansfield. His ancestors hailed from Scotland and legend has it that they were invited to leave that country because of sheep-killing activities! Alfred was a clever man who always had time for his fellow workers. At the time of his retirement he was the Toolroom Inspector, assisted by Walter Quible.

Before entering local government, Alfred became immersed in Trade Union activities after joining the Amalgamated Engineering Union in 1917. He was appointed secretary of the Mansfield Branch in 1940 and served continuously in that position for thirty-two years. Alfred staunchly supported the Trade Union movement for over fifty years.

During his time as a Borough Councillor he showed great enthusiasm, especially in the field of housing and became Chairman of the Housing Committee from 1948 to 1967. Under his guidance and because of his extensive knowledge of housing matters, the Ladybrook and Goodacre estates were completed. Alfred was instrumental in the opening of 'Sunnycroft' and 'Woodlands,' the first accommodation for the elderly of its type in the country. He also inaugurated the old persons' bungalow system in Mansfield. In addition, he was responsible for the first community building provided by the Mansfield Borough Council - Armstrong Hall on the Bull Farm estate.

In recognition of his work on the Housing and many

other committees, Alfred received the Freedom of the Borough in 1972, a well-deserved honour.

Over the years the company has boasted some of the finest engineers in the county and one of them, William Bull was the Toolroom foreman at Mansfield. He was tall, hailed from Carlisle and lived to be 100 years old. 'Bill' Bull, as he was known, was an experienced engineer who commanded respect from workers and management alike. Although a rather placid, religious person he was a strong disciplinarian and he received many plaudits from his fellow-members of the Society of Engineers at the functions held to celebrate his eightieth, ninetieth and one hundredth birthdays.

William was followed by George Davin, also a member of the Society of Engineers. George was a toolmaker by trade who had worked for Barlow Bros. at Hackney and Croydon and he spoke with a broad Cockney accent. A different personality to William, he was a short man with a quiet nature, but he did not mince words when things were not going well and kept a close eye on Toolroom operations. George was a skilled engineer and a capable foreman who was strict but fair in his judgement. He earned the respect of the Toolroom staff, some of who found him intimidating.

Jack Selby, another long-serving employee at Rock Valley, joined the company from Hudson Scott of Carlisle and lived on Westfield Lane, Mansfield. He was a time served engineer and a very good supervisor. Jack was in charge of the Talcum Department, which at that time was sited in the area now occupied by the offices and Medical Centre. It was later moved to part of the Press Shop and then to the top floor of the Tower Block. Jack, popular with staff and colleagues, was assisted diligently for many years by his forewoman, Hilda Scothern. He died at the age of ninety-six.

Below the Toy Factory was sited Bert Priddy's department that reminded one of Hades, as it contained tanks of bubbling, evil-smelling liquid, which cloaked the room in a steamy haze. The process was the recycling of tinplate, which was immersed in a caustic soda solution with a low voltage electrical current passed through it. This allowed the re-use of printed tinplate that had blemishes or scratch marks, or was surplus to orders. When the paint had been stripped off, the tinplate sheets were returned to the stores for re-issue. Bert, and his team of around seven girls, must have had a strong constitution to work in such conditions. Not only had they to contend with the smelly atmosphere, but they had to stand on duck-boards with water running beneath. This department was also responsible for electro-plating, mainly on advertising novelties, but also on caskets. Copper, brass, matt silver and nickel plating was carried out

In later years Bernard Toder took over the department, assisted by Dorothy, whose surname cannot be recalled. Eventually the department closed down, possibly due to Health and Safety requirements and the room was converted to a store.

The Toy Factory was the starting point for three long-serving ladies - Eva Shaw, who is currently living in retirement at the age of ninety-three, Dorothy Smith, who is mentioned later, and Polly Sipson. Polly was forewoman when the department was under the control of Harry Walker and Ralph Score was in the departmental office.

Another lady in a responsible position during the nineteen-thirties was Martha Truscott. She was the Female Superintendent and her domain covered the complete factory. A first-class leader and a good, practical disciplinarian, she could be tender-hearted towards her staff and operatives when necessary. In those days her female charges were known as 'Barringer's Angels.'

In this period before the Second World War, at around 7 am to 7-30am on weekday and Saturday mornings, Rock Valley and the surrounding roads were crowded as employees poured into the factory. Those travelling by rail from Ollerton, Edwinstowe, Bolsover, Nottingham and a multitude of intermediate stations, joined the throng. Rock Valley resounded with clattering feet, loud chatter and laughter. At the end of the day's work the whole process was reversed, probably with more laughter!

So used to this daily ritual, the employees would probably give scant attention to the impressive sycamore tree that stood near the main entrance to the factory. It was quite a landmark, which unfortunately is no longer there.

Two notable engineers left the company in the early nineteen-thirties, namely John Boneham and Albert Whiteley. Both became involved with well-known Mansfield firms that are still in business to this day. John Boneham became a partner in Boneham and Turners, Precision Engineers and Albert Whiteley began the Whiteley Radio Company. 'Whiteley's,' as it is known, later opened a cabinet works on Church Lane, Mansfield, which was eventually closed in order to concentrate on the electrical side of the business.

1939 to 1945

This period, which covers the Second World War years was a time of munitions work, air raids and food rationing. In 1939 Barringer Wallis and Manners became part of the Metal Box Company and the two factories were largely devoted to the manufacture of components to help in the war effort. These consisted of munitions components, respirators, mess tins and emergency ration containers. At Oddicroft Lane a section of the factory was run by B.S.A. (British Small Arms Company) whose personnel were employed on the manufacture of gun parts and jig tooling. This concentration on 'war work' meant that the absorption into the Metal Box Company had little impact on the day to day running of the factories.

It should be stressed that, despite the concentration on essential munitions work, many employees were drafted into the services and others were on deferment. Sadly, some of those who were called up failed to return, such as Len Hopkinson and Dick Brewin, both of whom had worked in the offices. Doubtless there were others who were equally unfortunate. I too served in the armed forces and would be gratified to see their names recorded in a roll of honour sited within the factory. (Lest we forget).

Many factory personnel were called upon to do their bit in Civil Defence. The Home Guard battalion was brought into line by ex-sergeant major Charlie Kilminster, who was the Factory Commissionaire at that time. A splendid uniformed figure, he was equally impressive on the parade ground, (the tennis court was commandeered for this purpose) with a commanding voice that could be heard as far away as Mansfield Market Place.

Fire-watching and plane-spotting were taken very seriously. For daytime purposes a concrete bunker was constructed on the rocks overlooking the Rock Valley Works and watch was maintained by Len Tooke and Captain Parker, whose contracts had been terminated by the Artists' Department, due to wartime restrictions. Night patrols were carried out by a small squad of male employees, who covered the factory sites in pairs. They were each armed with a rifle and two rounds of ammunition, with which to shoot on sight any German intruders! None were ever encountered and the only time a bullet was fired was when Norman Naggington let off a round accidentally in the section of the Toy Factory that was used as their sleeping quarters. One can imagine that a few choice words were uttered at the incident!

However, the much-appreciated reward for a night's duty was a huge breakfast comprising the luxury of eggs and bacon, served by the Canteen Manageress. Each man would eat as much as possible, bearing in mind the meal was equivalent to a family's ration for a week!

Bill Saxton was one of the employees who witnessed the concentration on 'war work.' He began his employment with Barringer Wallis and Manners some years earlier as an engineer and he gave many years of loyal service. Prior to the war period he had taken charge of the I.B.U. Department and he ran the production side of the Rock Valley factory for the duration of the war. On many occasions he worked until 10pm and, on Fridays he paid the wages to the production staff. In later years Bill acquired the nickname of 'Bulging Bill,' which arose from his work on a process invented by Seth Fortune and Arthur Dove, at the Oddicroft Lane factory. It consisted of bulging round containers into a barrel shape using centrifugal force. A prototype machine was built for the purpose and when it went into production it was Bill who set it up and maintained it. Bill's nickname became so widely known that a rack in the Tool Store, dedicated to tools used in the bulging operation, was identified with the name 'Bulging Bill!'

A person who deserves special recognition for his efforts during the troubled times of the Second World War is Bill Naylor, a member of the office staff. He kept in touch with the employees who were serving in the armed forces and he edited a Forces Newsletter, which was issued to them and provided news from home. There may well be some of these Newsletters still in existence.

1945 to 1983

The end of the Second World War brought considerable change to the company. The Head Office of the Metal Box Company appointed a General Manager to take control of the Mansfield and Sutton-in-Ashfield sites. This appointment brought Kenneth McLean to Mansfield, who it is believed, worked for Gray Dunn's of Glasgow prior to joining the Metal Box Company. Although new to tin box making, he had the personality, drive and flair ideally suited to the Barringer Wallis and Manners philosophy.

The management team under Kenneth McLean at this time is believed to be as follows:

Factory Manager, Mansfield	- D.B.Huffam
Works Manager, Mansfield	- G.F.Gledhill
Branch Commercial Manager	- L.G.Wass
Branch Buying Manager	- S.Bills
Branch Quality Controller	- B.Reynolds
Branch Production Controller	- R.Mitchell
Branch Personnel Officer	- A. Wilson
Branch Chief Engineer	- W.H.Beadsmore
Factory Manager, Sutton-in-Ashfield	- W.Ormston
Works Manager, Sutton-in-Ashfield	- W.H.Walker

Kenneth McLean had created new positions, such as Production Controller, Quality Controller and Personnel Officer. Many of the above were existing employees and the General Manager's faith in them ensured their wholehearted co-operation and effort, which was invaluable during the extensive re-organisation of the Mansfield and Sutton-in-Ashfield sites that took place after the war. A Functional Management Team was established and control was exercised by means of a short daily management meeting, normally held at 10am but occasionally supplemented by breakfast meetings. It took the form of a short question and answer session, referred to as 'Q.A.'

The enthusiastic, open style of Kenneth McLean broke down barriers that had existed between the management, offices and shop floor workers. He toured the Mansfield factory every morning and got to know many of the staff and impressed on them his maxim, 'only the best will do.' Any manager or employee who went on business for the company was always accommodated in a first-class hotel and given expenses to match. They were instructed to act as a diplomat for their employer and entertain their guests, or contacts to the highest standard. His interest in the employees' activities was considerable and he encouraged involvement in local political affairs as it provided publicity, very important for the company image.

True to Kenneth McLean's Scottish origins, he named his house on Park Avenue, Mansfield, 'Lochbuie.' In later years it became a small hotel, run by the company, for Head Office employees and customers paying short and, occasionally, long visits to the factories. Eventually it was taken over by the Local Authority to provide accommodation for the homeless.

D.B.Huffam, Factory Manager, was an up and coming young man who eventually replaced Kenneth McLean as General Manager on his retirement. Well-educated and highly respected, he visited the production departments regularly, keeping in constant touch with many of the staff. He was a true Metal Box man destined for higher things. Eventually promoted to Head Office he rose to become a main board director of the Metal Box Company

George Gledhill, Works Manager, joined the Mansfield Management from Hull and, together with George Townsend, assisted by Walter H. Walker, at Sutton-in-Ashfield, ran the production side of the business. George

Gledhill displayed an air of confidence and had a voice that was instantly recognisable. A very sociable person, he would always acknowledge employees whenever he met them, but he was not wholly in favour of craftsmen in positions of authority, such as departmental supervisors, or superintendents, as the senior ones were called at the time. As time progressed container-making machinery had became more sophisticated and required expert knowledge to run and maintain output. More and more engineers had been appointed to these posts but, due to a change in company policy, the supervisory structure was reorganised and the position of superintendent was discontinued. This did not please the people who held that position, for they looked upon promotion as a step into management, be it technical or otherwise. Bill Saxton was particularly put out, having run the production side of the factory during the Second World War and proved himself a reliable and conscientious superintendent. Despite his disappointment, Bill remained loyal to the company and to illustrate this, I relate an episode that occurred one Sunday around noon. I was on my way to Mansfield Market Place to buy a Sunday newspaper, which, at that time was sold outside Burton's tailors. I had arranged to meet Bill Chamberlain (a friend from the Toolroom) and, after obtaining a newspaper I met him at the bottom of Leeming Street. We saw Bill Saxton approaching, raincoat over his arm and smoking a pipe. He was obviously coming from the factory and heading for the Nottingham Road bus stop in the Market Square, to make his way home. William and I invited Bill to join us for a drink in the Swan Hotel and his reply was somewhat surprising. 'I'm sorry, but I must return to work after lunch, you see. I feel that I want to grow old with the firm.' Such was Bill's devotion to the company.

George Gledhill bore no animosity towards Bill Saxton and the engineers in general. In fact, on his many visits to the factory from the Isle of Skye, where he lived in retirement, George would always visit the Toolroom to chat to the engineers he knew. After his demotion Bill Saxton returned to the Toolroom to join the tool repair section and was soon promoted to charge-hand. Unfortunately he suffered tragic family losses and lived alone for the final twenty years of his life. A sad situation for a true gentleman to endure.

George Townsend, George Gledhill's counterpart at Sutton-in Ashfield, was a competent manager who was held in high esteem by all his employees. Under his guidance the day to day running of the production departments was relatively trouble free and harmonious.

Sidney (Sid) Bills became Branch Buying Manager, when Frank Maltby retired. Frank was an old Barringer Wallis and Manners employee and brother to the director, William Maltby. The supply of tinplate was one of Sid's responsibilities in addition to ensuring that production was not interrupted by shortage of materials. He was a dedicated pipe smoker and a very pleasant person, who lived on Sutton Road, Mansfield. Sid enjoyed watching cricket in his leisure time and was a season ticket holder at Trent Bridge, home of Nottinghamshire C.C.C. On his many visits there he was sometimes accompanied by Sid Clarke, Fred Renshaw, Charles Fletcher and Dorothy M. Brooks.

For practical purposes the remaining employees during the period 1945-1983 are grouped by department, or senior management position, as they represent the majority of those that are recalled. The number of employees had grown from approximately fifty, in 1895 to 2,600 at the end of the Second World War.

General Manager

C.W.Parkinson replaced D.B.Huffam in 1955 after serving roughly twelve months as Factory Manager, Mansfield. He joined the Metal Box Company as a trainee direct from university (Cambridge), being initially attached to the Dairycoates Factory at Hull. In 1939 he was transferred to the Metal Box Company (Overseas Division) in India, as a member of the Sales Department at the Bombay Factory. During the Second World War he served in the R.I.N.V.R. for five years, before returning to Bombay at the end of the war. In 1948 he was promoted to Manager of the Bombay factory. Returning to England in 1954 he took up the position of Factory Manager at Rock Valley. In just over a year he rose to become General Manager of Mansfield and Sutton-in-Ashfield before being appointed to the Head Office post of General Line Group Manager. A remarkable advancement.

His style of management differed from that of his predecessors in that he delegated more and paid fewer visits to the factory production departments. Personally I got on with him very well and he interviewed me on a number of occasions when I applied to join the Overseas Division of the Metal Box Company. On those occasions I found his first-hand knowledge of working overseas very useful. Despite his tenure at Mansfield being extraordinarily brief, I have pleasant memories of that period.

The next incumbent was C.I.Mellor, a flamboyant, though softly spoken gentleman. Extremely well-educated, he took a deep interest in the Mansfield and Sutton-in-Ashfield factories and was very much 'hands on' in all aspects of the business. A resolute driving force for progress, he questioned many existing practices and control systems and he was the first General Manager to be involved at first hand in the design and promotion of new products. So much so that he became renowned for coming into the factory on his arrival in a morning with a prototype model, or drawing of a container that he had cobbled together in the garage at his home in Southwell! It is reckoned that he drove John Scott, of the Commercial Department, mad at times with his insistence that an idea of his should be sent for costing and for Arthur Dove, or myself to produce a working model, prior to estimates for tooling being prepared. It was then John Scott's task to progress this information.

It must be conceded that many of these ideas were good and eventually went into production. One that I particularly liked was a double-shell waiter tray, around twelve inches in diameter, with three removable, brass-plated legs, a really practical concept. Initiative of this kind was a great asset to our product range and I found him very easy to talk to on this subject. He inspired more new ideas and products than any of his predecessors.

All the employees found him a to be good leader and easy

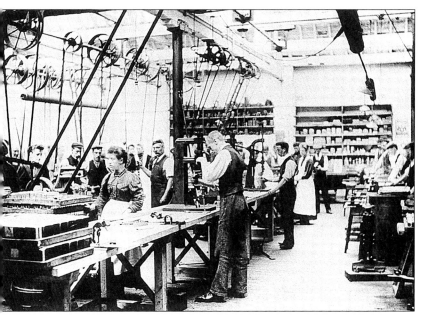

The 'Making Department,' Rock Valley Works, in the early 1900's

The Old Press Shop, Rock Valley Works, in the early 1900's

The Old Print Room and Stores, in the early 1900's

A Production Line in I.B.U. Department, in the early 1900's

Frontage of Rock Valley Works, around 1912

Exhibition of Barringer Wallis and Manners products, in 1914

William Holmes Reddan with Queen Mary in the Artist' Studio, in 1914

Gathering of employees outside Rock Valley Works during the visit of King George V and Queen Mary, in 1914

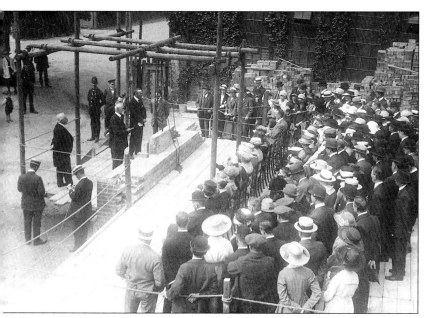

Laying of the Foundation Stone for
Tower Block, Mansfield, in 1919

Directors and their wives attending the
Foundation Stone Laying, in 1919

*Girls retouching the decoration of tins,
Rock Valley Works, in the 1930's*

*Mansfield Metal Box Apprentices' Adventure Club,
winter expedition*

*Mansfield Metal Box canteen staff and several employees,
around 1950*

*Mansfield and Sutton Metal Box Football Team that played in
the North Notts. Alliance League, in the early 1960's*

Mansfield Engineers Football Team, in the 1950's

Sutton Toolroom and Sutton Tool-setters
Football Teams, in 1960

to get on with, for he was always concerned about their welfare and progress. He justly earned their respect and also that of his superiors for he was eventually rewarded by being appointed General Line Group Manager and became a director on the main board. I believe he was the longest-serving General Manager of the Mansfield and Sutton-in-Ashfield factories.

Ronald Westbrook, who lived on Lichfield Lane, Mansfield, came to Rock Valley as General Manager after service with the Metal Box Company (Overseas Division) in India, emulating C.W.Parkinson. Mr Westbrook must rank as one of the most popular General Managers and he was just the person needed at that time to boost morale. He was a dignified and honest man who stuck to his word and freely admitted if he was wrong. Fair in his judgement he treated all employees as equals in his efforts to maintain the high standard to which he aspired.

Ronald Westbrook kept in daily contact with all departments and developed a good system of communication. He encouraged Sports and Social activities and could always be seen at employee functions within the factories or at parties elsewhere. Together with John Watts, the Personnel Manager at that time, he took a keen interest in the activities of the branch pensioners and on his retirement he chaired their committee meetings. All visitors to the company were made welcome, particularly the local civic dignitaries on their annual visits. Mr Westbrook encouraged staff participation in local politics, for which the company offered generous time off with pay for civic duties. From a Trade Union standpoint he was an honest negotiator whose word was his bond.

When Ronald Westbrook retired in 1974, after forty-two years' service with the Metal Box Company, he was succeeded by Alan Russell. After joining the Leicester branch of the company, Mr Russell moved to Head Office in 1960, to become Head of Quality Control for the General Line Group. His next appointment was Works Manager at the Carlisle branch, where he eventually became General Manager. In 1971 he was transferred to Mansfield as Factory Manager before filling the post vacated by Ronald

Westbrook.

Alan Russell's style of management, once again, differed from his predecessors' and, due to several factors, company activity began to slow down. Competition from other forms of packaging began to have an effect and the stigma of redundancy raised its head. Confidence was not boosted by the fact that evening shift and overtime working was reduced. After a short spell in charge Alan Russell returned to Head Office, but sadly, was forced to take early retirement due to ill health. However, I am happy to relate that he has made an excellent recovery and now lives in Leicestershire.

His replacement, Alan Robson had progressed through the commercial side of the business and his tenure was also brief. Under a reorganisation of the General Line Group of the Metal Box Company, he was transferred to the closure factory at Bridge of Allan, in Scotland, as General Manager. Before retirement Alan spent some years as a consultant within the tin-box making industry.

Factory Manager

The aforementioned Eddie Walsh succeeded George Gledhill. His first position had been Office Junior in the Transport Department before periods spent in the Commercial and Production Control Departments. The latter department was run at that time by R. Mitchell. After military service during the Second World War, Eddie returned to the Production Control Department and when R.Mitchell left Eddie took charge of the department, breathing life into it and keeping everyone on their toes. Despite his energetic approach he was popular with his staff and work colleagues who saw him as able, sincere and fair.

On the retirement of George Gledhill, Eddie was promoted to the post of Factory Manager. He had a good pedigree, having worked his way up from the grass roots to senior management. His office door, (or window) was always open, there were no barriers. I mention window because at one period it acted as his office entrance! Like Ronald Westbrook, Eddie was always willing to participate in any factory celebration and at Christmas he, along with other members of the management team, would visit all departments to thank the employees for their efforts over the past year and to wish them the compliments of the season. Eddie was a staunch Roman Catholic who was glad to retain Good Friday as a factory holiday for many years and fish was always on the menu on Fridays during his tenure.

Eddie left Mansfield to become General Manager of the Company's two factories in Hull, but little time had elapsed before he was asked to take charge of a factory in Nigeria, owned by the Metal Box (Overseas Division). Eventually Eddie returned to Hull, where, I believe, he remained until retirement. Despite his roving commission during his latter years with the company, I think, deep down, Mansfield was always home to Eddie.

Following Eddie Walsh's departure to Hull, Noel Fenton became Factory Manager at Mansfield. He was a pleasant, popular person who married another employee, Audrey (?). He died, sadly, whilst still in his fifties.

Bert Moakes, who had risen through the Drawing Office to become Chief Design Engineer, became Noel Fenton's successor, but he too, died comparatively young.

Employees

We now move to the division of employees by department, commencing at the far end of the Rock Valley site.

Toy Factory

The ladies that I recall who worked in this old building are identified on page twenty-five.

Press Shop

In the early days the presses in this department were driven by line shafting and pulleys, which created much noise. They were used for the stamping out of components, such as lids and canister ends, embossed casket bodies and also trays. Harry Childs supervised the department assisted by K. Holmes and Florence Beech, forewoman. Jess Farmilo was the departmental engineer, Sid Clarke and Herbert Baggaley were tool-setters and all three of them eventually moved on to more senior positions.

Later Polly Sipson became forewoman and two of the operatives I recall were Ethell Plume and Sybil Reeves. Harry Childs took control of a small area in the centre of the factory, on the ground floor, which housed the heavy friction presses used for embossing large body strips. The female operators were required to sit in a well in order to operate these very tall presses and it was very heavy work. Following acquisitions by the Metal Box Company the Press Shop began the production of hardware items, such as bread bins, coal boxes incorporating a folding scoop, pedal bins, a range of kitchen canisters, waste paper bins, waiter trays, table trays with folding legs, bathroom items, table mats and coasters. Most of these items were made from heavier gauge metal, which required the use of the large, heavy-duty presses.

Additional staff was recruited and shift working was introduced to cope with the influx of extra trade. By this time the department was under the control of Sid Clarke, assisted by Herbert Baggaley, as charge-hand. The tool-setters, more numerous now, were Dennis Quinton, George Haywood, Doug Holland, Bob Reynolds, George Greenwood and 'Polish George,' as he was nicknamed. In the Press Shop office were Gwen Lane (Wakeling), forewoman, Ida Frisby, charge-hand, Eileen Briggs, and Joan Bramwell.

Herbert Baggaley eventually took over the running of the department. Very experienced in all areas of presswork, Herbert was a hard, but fair taskmaster, noted for his plain speaking and dislike of bureaucracy. A true 'character,' he always had a story to tell and he liked to address all male employees as 'Charlie,' irrespective of their position, which, on one occasion included the General Manager, by mistake! The recipient of this description, C.I. Mellor, had occasion to ring Herbert shortly afterwards and displayed his sense of humour by introducing himself as 'Charlie' Mellor!

Herbert played a major role in getting off the ground the high-speed production lines that were to produce millions of small hardware items sold as premium gifts. During his latter years he transferred to the Production Control Department and acted in an advisory capacity. His wide experience and common sense made him a good committee person. In his leisure time Herbert was a keen sportsman, an outstanding swimmer and water polo player.

Scott Williams took Herbert Baggaley's position in charge of the Press Shop, having gained supervisory experience in control of the Seamless Department. A Toolroom engineer by trade, he was known for his wisecracks and practical jokes. In his spare time he was an accomplished magician and a member of the Magic Circle. He was a very popular entertainer at the annual Childrens' Christmas Party run by the company and was a good cricketer, playing for Woodhouse Amateurs before joining the Mansfield Metal Box team. Like Herbert Baggaley before him, Scott eventually moved to the Production Control Department.

Jack Tyler then took over the Press Shop, having run the Talcum Department for several years. Jack also began his career with the company as a Toolroom engineer who spent a considerable time on a milling machine when he returned from war service in the Royal Navy. Like Scott Williams, Jack was popular with his fellow employees and entertained the children at the Christmas Parties. He was keen on amateur dramatics and starred for many years in the annual Westfield Folk House Pantomimes, being especially remembered for his performance as 'Widow Twanky.' Later Jack became a member, and eventually chairman, of the Mansfield Operatic Society. A few years after becoming the Press Shop supervisor, Jack retired.

Slitting

The area vacated in the Press Shop by the Talcum Department when it moved to the Tower Block was taken over by the tinplate slitting section. In charge initially was Arnold White, a long-serving member of the company and one of the superintendents together with Jack Selby, Jack Horsefield and Bill Saxton. He was soon followed by Lou Houseley who was transferred from Sutton-in-Ashfield. New machines were brought in to meet increased demand and the department worked to full capacity. The charge-hand was Lol Hepworth, also from Sutton-in-Ashfield and the machine setters were Gus Witts, N.Wilson and Terry Brown. Florence Walker was forewoman, a spinster who lived with her sister, who also worked at the factory, in the Ravensdale area of Mansfield. 'Floss' as she was known was a kind person, not as strict as her counterparts, but she knew her job and ensured that the department was kept clean and tidy. Jean Cantrill followed Florence as forewoman and was a real success, being very knowledgeable in all aspects of the operations. Jean was so accomplished, she would have been competent as a supervisor, but she was also always ready for a laugh. Margaret Pickering, one of the natural blond sisters that worked at the factory, ran the section office. Sadly, she died aged seventy-four, in 1999.

Irregular Built Up (IBU)

This canister and casket-making department was very labour intensive, but was always busy producing tea caddies and fancy biscuit tins. Heavily embossed caskets, often fitted with locks were a feature of this department, which played a vital roll during the coronation year of 1953 when the production lines were working flat out until 10pm each evening and on Saturday morning. The workforce put in a tremendous effort.

In charge in the early days was Jack Horsefield, a superintendent at that time. He was followed by Bill Saxton, Horace Ashton, Doug Holland and John Truman. The male support staff I recall was George Spencer, W. Haque, Jack Fletcher, Everret Reeves, George Ruth, Joe Evans, Bram Willaby, John Froggat, Jim McHugh, Chris Bowler and R.Reynolds. The forewoman was Sue Massey, who later emigrated to America and joined the Church of the Latter Day Saints, (Mormon) in the State of Utah. Her sister, Cissie Massey had succeeded Martha Truscott as Female Superintendent. Dorothy Bagnall took over Sue's position on her departure and she was extremely strict. It was not unusual to see tears being shed by the female operatives after Dorothy had discovered some misdemeanour. It is true to say that she had no favourites amongst her girls. When Dorothy retired Sue Massey took over once more, having just returned from America. Surprisingly, Sue never married and when she retired, Dorothy Cooke, who became very popular with all the employees in the department, was her replacement. Female charge-hand at one period was Mary Carrington.

Worcester Ware

In 1964 the Metal Box Company closed their Providence Works at Worcester and the bulk of their Hardware business, known as 'Worcester Ware,' was transferred to Mansfield. As mentioned previously, the majority of this production was carried out in the Press Shop, but at the time of its transfer, a small assembly section was set up in the area between the Press Shop and the $9\frac{1}{4}$ Line. It was supervised by Jim Ashley who had worked at Providence Works. He was a very conscientious and hardworking person who took his job very seriously, but it did take him some time to come to terms with the modifications to the production methods introduced at Mansfield. Jim unfortunately died within a few years of his transfer. Later, this area was used for the storage of Worcester Ware items.

$9\frac{1}{4}$ Line

This department was so called because of its production of $9\frac{1}{4}$ inch square margarine tins. It was often referred to as the 'Bread and Butter Line.' Waste paper bins were also manufactured in this department whilst it was under the supervision of Joe Longden, assisted by Irene Richardson. Tool-setters on this line were Reg Wilson and Bob Reynolds.

An area adjacent to this production line was always referred to as 'Trafalgar Square.' It contained two fountains with large bowls, used for hand-washing prior to going to the canteen. Beyond the $9\frac{1}{4}$ line were stairs leading to the following departments in the Tower Block

Seamless

This department was also known as the 'Players Room,' because it housed the production lines manufacturing tobacco tins, mainly with solid-drawn bodies and lids, hence the name 'Seamless.' Some tins were of the locked-corner variety, requiring skilled tooling and operation. At one time only two toolmakers at the factory could make the press tools to produce the fine tolerances that this type of tin demanded. Millions of tobacco tins were produced for such well-known brands as Players Navy Cut, Senior Service, Capstan, Park Drive, WD and HO Wills Gold Flake, Lambert and Butler and Gallaghers.

Arnold White ran the department at one time. He was a very skilled engineer, keen on D.I.Y. in his leisure time. On his retirement he moved to Hythe, on the edge of the New Forest and I often visited him and enjoyed a social drink. Later Scott Williams became the supervisor and he was followed by Roger Flint, a Toolroom engineer. Eventually, John Truman, who ran several departments over the years, took over. Tool-setters were Bernard Allen, 'Nobby' Clarke, Cyril Repton, Reg England and Bill Simpson. Forewoman was Phyllis Broadhead, a very tall lady and very strict with the girls in her charge. Quite late in life she married Bill Rose who was the supervisor in the Tinplate Store. They lived close to the factory, on Recreation Street. Phyllis was succeeded by Dorothy Smith.

Fancy Box

This department occupied the middle floor of the Tower Block and was also referred to as 'Fancy Box and Advertising.' Like IBU, it was very labour intensive and a variety of fancy-shaped embossed containers, of high quality, were manufactured, in addition to coffee and tea caddies, toffee tins and caskets. Amongst numerous other products were toy novelties, advertising notepads with embossed covers, often copper or nickel-plated. Advertising plaques in varying sizes were fabricated, such as Michelin Forecourt maps and tyre-pressure charts. These plaques were two foot by three foot in dimension and had to be manhandled by the female operatives on the folding machines, no easy task. Shelf strips advertising toothpaste etc. were also produced, but the most complicated product was the counter dispenser used for dispensing packets of sweets, chewing gum, carnation corn caps and the like. Small tins for holding Iron Jelloids, Little Imps and snuff were made, mainly from aluminium and of riveted construction.

In charge of this department was Jim McHugh, who, you will recall was a die-setter in IBU. A tall man, Jim had a very pleasant disposition and was very knowledgeable. He always took part in factory social events and enjoyed playing bowls. Jim was a member of the Mansfield Bowling Club, which, I believe, played on Westfield Lane, not far from Jim's home on Beck Crescent. His forewoman was Dorothy Smith, another person who was very strict with her girls. She must have frightened the younger ones to death, but she had a gentler side to her nature. If she was aware of any hardship or misfortune amongst her staff she ensured that they were well cared for.

One person who particularly deserves a mention is a charge-hand, Ann Holloway, a spinster who was exceptionally pleasant to everyone. She was ready to help any girl in trouble, often at the expense of risking discipline from Dorothy Smith. Very seldom reporting any misdemeanours if she thought she could resolve the situation on the spot, Ann was a true friend to her girls, but also firm and just towards them. On her retirement the entire department laid on a first-class celebration in her honour and, I believe, for the first time in her life she nearly got drunk! During Ann's long retirement she often spoke of the event with affection and mirth. A wonderful person, she died at the ripe old age of eighty-eight.

Tool-setters in the department were Thomas Radford, charge-hand, Chris Bowler, Dennis Quinton and Ken Henson. A later trend was the transfer of tool-setters to other departments, as and when required, and some on a more permanent basis. For example, Ken Henson was transferred to Talcum Department to work with Jack Selby and Tony Childs. Such labour transfers frequently happened when production lines were re-sighted in other departments.

Talcum
Following several earlier moves, this department was sited

on the top floor of the Tower Block. Jack Selby remained in charge for several years with Hilda Scothern as his forewoman. Jack was replaced by the versatile John Truman and. Hilda Scothern's replacement was Olive Mills, with Elsie Johnson as her charge-hand. Jack Tyler eventually took over the department and ran it for a number of years before moving to take charge of the Press Shop.

Extrusion

This department was housed in a building across the road from the main factory. It was mentioned in the Introduction that during the late nineteen-forties the extrusion process was in its infancy. The person responsible for making it into a profitable part of the company was Howard Dugdale, an accomplished engineer who understood the complexities of aluminium extrusion and ran the department for many years. A familiar feature of the extrusion process became instantly recognisable to the factory employees. It was the distinctive smell caused by the heat generated when the heavy press tool impacted on a lubricated aluminium slug, thereby forming a long thin-walled tube.

Howard's first large order was for what was known as the 'Latex Bowl,' used by rubber tree tappers for the collection of latex sap that the tree produced. This product was produced successfully and was followed by orders for radio components, pharmaceutical tubes, cigar tubes, film tubes and later, aerosol containers and toothpaste tubes for Gibbs Ltd.

The department also housed its own print lines and the person in charge of these was Tommy Allen, a time-served printer who was very experienced in this type of process and loved to tell everyone how he had solved any problems that arose in his line of work. Tommy was very accomplished and extremely loyal to the company. A sociable man, he took part in all such activities and was greatly involved in fundraising for local charitable causes.

Harry Marsh was deputy to Howard Dugdale until he took over the department after Howard's retirement. He was quiet and studious with very fixed ideas, but he got on with his staff and was a good committee person. The forewoman was Phyllis Ball who lived on Newgate Lane, Mansfield and was held in high regard by her female operatives. She married a machine operator who also worked in the department

Transport

The previously mentioned Frank Clarke retired during the early post war years after a long spell in charge. He was replaced by Bill Rose, who was followed in turn by Charlie Harris.

In anticipation of William Pallisser's retirement from the garage, Stanley (Stan) Bellamy joined the department as chauffeur. He gained a reputation as a first-class employee, being Rolls Royce trained and a superb ambassador for the company. Stan was a gentleman's gentleman, highly capable of conversing with anyone he transported, be it Head Office directors, important customers or factory employees. The same courtesy was extended to all as they were driven to bus or train station, or to the Sutton-in-Ashfield site. He was sadly missed when he retired and it was pleasing to see the respect paid to him by senior management on the sad occasion of his death after a long retirement. This ex-guardsman and his wife, who also worked at the Mansfield factory were never forgotten by those who worked with them.

Stan was replaced by Dennis Kent, a reserved and religious person, but very pleasant and helpful. He married the daughter of Edward (Ted) Backus, an engineer in the Toolroom.

The lorry drivers I remember were Reg Ward, Ernest Welch, Alfred Holland and Lou Truscott, acting as 'driver's mate.'

Despatch

Earlier reference was made to a small Press Shop sited in the Despatch Department, adjacent to IBU, where items were manufactured for the 'stock box' range. This section was later used for stamping lids and bottoms for containers made in IBU. It was called into service once more in 1962, when the General Line manufacture was transferred from

Sutton-in-Ashfield, to produce certain components and also Robinson's caps.

The tool-setters, who transferred along with the General Line business were John Horn, Ron (Space) Davies and Horace Barker. They were very skilled and speedy workers and a pleasure to work with.

It was in this area that the fork lift trucks were housed and their operators were Tommy Friend, Joe Baxter, a small person, always cheerful and Freddie Gant who acted as Convenor of the TGWU at the factory. Ray Collins was also a member of the team, a talented pianist who often played the piano for departmental parties and similar celebrations with Leslie Pinder, a member of the Mansfield Operatic Society. They made a very entertaining duo.

Harry Farmer was in charge of Despatch during the 1950's and 1960's and the staff at that time consisted of Roy Hart, Madge Everest, Harry Hind and Edna Broughton

Quality Control

This department was given a very important impetus following the Second World War when a Quality Controller was appointed by Kenneth McLean. Each department had a quality control female staff member and components were examined on a batch basis. Tests were also carried out on materials, printed plate and finished articles. Barry Reynolds was initially in charge of the department, followed later by Walter Walker and then Ernest Dakin. Support staff included Mick Smith, who sadly, passed away in 1999, sisters Annie and Doris Hursthouse, Maisy Bradbury, Doris Dring, Edith Dring, Shirley Burdett and Flora Banner. These employees formed a highly skilled and conscientious team.

Engineering - Chief Engineers and Assistants

Howard Beadsmore held the position of Chief Engineer until his retirement in the 1960's. He was a good, all-round engineer who was also a skilled blacksmith, spending his early working life at a local colliery. Especially knowledgeable regarding factory maintenance, he was a very accomplished landscape gardener in his non-working hours. Howard was a dedicated member of the local Baptist Church and lived at Larch Farm and Cuckney.

His replacement was Cyril Bull who transferred from the Hull branch of The Metal Box Company. Cyril played a major roll in the modernisation of factory production methods by innovating and designing tools and plant to meet increased demand. He should take credit for the introduction of new, long-term products that were a real asset to the business. An engineer of exceptional quality, Cyril was greatly respected by all in the engineering field and factory management, the captain of a great ship. Living in the Berry Hill area of Mansfield for a number of years, he eventually moved, some time after his retirement, to Surrey in order to be near his immediate family.

John Adams was a very talented Assistant Chief Engineer who served under Howard Beadsmore. He was a man of ideas and foresight who eventually moved to the Plastics Division. His replacement was John Bennett, another accomplished employee.

Assistant Chief Engineer under Cyril Bull was Albert Newton, who moved from Sutton-in-Ashfield at the time of the transfer of General Line production. Albert experienced a period of considerable change and he was closely involved with the soudronically welded containers and commercial industrial pressings aspect of the business. He also maintained close contact with the Drawing Office regarding design and development of new tools and processes. Albert became Chief Engineer when Cyril Bull retired and was still in the post in 1983.

Engineering - Toolroom

Howard Stordy succeeded George Davin as Toolroom Supervisor in the early 1950's. Initially hard to get on with, it was a case of a new man with a different personality and methods. It was also a time of upheaval due to the introduction of the hardware range. The unfamiliar tooling and production methods used for 'Worcester Ware' and the demand for faster production throughputs put pressure on Howard and the toolmakers under his control. Nevertheless, I got along with him through what, I think, was a mixture of mutual respect for our different crafts and compromise. I wonder how many engineers remember his unforgettable phrase, delivered in broad local slang - 'Yo be reight wi' me and I'll be reight wi' yo!'

One person Howard could never fathom was Ted Parnham, an engineer who moved from Sheepbridge Stokes and lived with his parents at the Bramley Arms public house beside the River Trent at Fiskerton Ferry. Very rarely did Ted arrive at work on time (7-30am), for he had to cross a main railway line at a level crossing and invariably its gates were closed. In consequence Ted frequently did not put in an appearance until after 7-45am. One morning, at 8-05am, Howard observed Ted Parnham at his bench, having a snack and shaving with an electric razor. Unknown to him, Ted had clocked in a few minutes previously but was 'quartered,' which meant he would only be paid from 8-15am. Howard shot from his elevated office, his progress followed by an audience full of anticipation for what was to come. Arriving at Ted's bench Howard barked, 'Ted, you should have been here at 7-30am!' to which Ted replied calmly, 'Why? What happened? Howard was taken aback until Ted pointed out that he was not obliged to start work until 8-15am and that it was customary for him to work a shorter lunch hour to make up the lost time. Being new to the post of supervisor, Howard was not aware of this and had to make his peace with Ted. However, he must have been further irritated by Ted's performance during tours of the factory by visitors. As soon as the visiting party entered the Toolroom Ted would lie in the middle of the gangway, as though unconscious. One could not help laughing at the sight of shocked visitors stepping warily over Ted's inert body. Despite these tribulations Howard and Ted became good pals and Howard must have been greatly amused by an incident involving Ted outside of work. Ted was an accomplished sprinter and received the accolade of being picked to represent his county in the AAA's championships at the White City. Knowing he had no chance at all of winning and being the joker he was, Ted got no further than a few yards in the race before pulling up with a non-existent muscle strain and limping off the track! Eventually, Ted left the company to become manager of a local Odeon cinema, a job he retained until his retirement. Ted was one of many employees that made going to work a pleasure, a person guaranteed to make you laugh and brighten your working day.

Howard Stordy eventually moved to the estimating section of the Engineering Department and he was followed as supervisor by Harry Hurst, who had worked in the Toolroom for many years, some of his time being spent on a milling machine alongside Jack Tyler.

A particularly popular charge-hand under Howard Stordy was Horace Spencer, a kindly and even-tempered person who went out of his way to help the engineers in his charge.

Another Toolroom engineer with an interesting personality was Bill (Chick) Chamberlain, who has been mentioned earlier. He was a long-serving employee who was called to the colours in the First World War and served with the Sherwood Rangers, a Nottinghamshire cavalry regiment. He was slightly built, with just the right frame for a jockey. This possibly caused him to emulate one with his favourite routine of straddling the moving head of his shaping machine and riding it as though it was a horse. Always one for a joke, Bill would play a trick on unwary employees who happened to pass his machine. He would invite them to try his 'lung-tester,' a small cylinder with a rotating fan mounted on top of it. The unfortunate guinea pig was asked to blow into the two tubes protruding from the cylinder to see if they could rotate the fan. Chick would first give a demonstration but, unknown to the employee he placed his tongue over one of the tubes to prevent a fine film of black dust from emerging. When the unsuspecting employee blew into the cylinder he would invariably blow into both tubes causing the fine dust to spray on his upper lip. The engineers working on the surrounding machines and benches would struggle to keep a straight face as the poor recipient walked away sporting a handsome black moustache!

Bill was nonetheless a skilled machinist who loved to relate stories from his youth and wartime experiences. He was a true friend and he enjoyed a pint of 'Mansfield Mild' in the King's Arms throughout his working life. When he died, aged eighty-five, he was sadly missed by his former work-mates.

I often pause and think of other work colleagues, many of them characters in their own right. Here are some of those that I recall:

R.Gouk, who, I think, was related to the local family that had connections with the Mansfield Library from 1891 to 1935. He eventually left the company to join Huntley Bourne and Stevens of Reading.

Jess Farmilo, who, you will recall, married Freda Barrington and worked in the Toolroom for a period. He rose from the position of departmental engineer in the Press Shop to eventually take charge of the Drawing Office. An outspoken man he made his feelings felt on one occasion when he noticed that his car, parked outside the factory, was being tampered with. The perpetrator was mortified when Jess leaned out of the window and bellowed, 'Hey, you! Get off that * * * * * * * car!

Joe Greasley operated a shaping machine next to that of Bill Chamberlain. They became good friends but, unfortunately, in later life Joe suffered quite a severe stroke. However he was determined to resume work and the company arranged helpfully for him to work several afternoons per week. He could be seen making his way slowly to and from the factory despite retaining partial paralysis down one side of his body. Joe was provided with a stool at the side of his machine and I think having the company of his work-mates meant a lot to him.

Malcolm Marshall, a serious-minded toolmaker, was known for his eagerness and haste. One afternoon he was in the inspection department where a tank, containing oil that was used in the hardening process, was sited. Instead of waiting for the person employed on the hardening and tempering process he decided to do it himself. The proper procedure involved removing white-hot components from a furnace and immersing them in the tank of oil, utilising protective clothing, such as a visor, apron and gloves. Wearing only the gloves he lowered the heated components into the tank, but, unfortunately, did not completely immerse them, as procedure dictated The oil ignited and flames nearly engulfed Malcolm, who leapt away from the tank with hair singed, bright red face and glasses askew. He was not allowed to live down the unfortunate incident for some time!

Colin West was another character I recall. A lively and sociable person, he could be a bit of a rogue at times. He was a good fast bowler who played for Blidworth Welfare in a local cricket league.

Tools used for the embossing of components were in the main cut by hand with a wide range of special steel chisels. One person who specialised in this skill was Tommy Burton, a large man with a serious persona who would cover up his work and tools whenever anyone approached him. He was the only person to have this habit and the only one involved in his craft that did not have an apprentice.

Working at an adjacent bench was Vic Anderson, a colleague engaged on the same work. Vic could be short tempered and people had to approach him with caution. Nevertheless, he would always help his work-mates if required.

Many of the toolmakers had hobbies outside of work and one I recall in particular was Les Barrows, who lived at Calverton and was a keen rose-grower.

Alan Walton, another good toolmaker, left the company to run the Queen's Head public house in Worksop.

Ted Backus was very involved in Trade Union matters and he was Branch President for the AEU (Amalgamated Engineering Union), as it was known at that time. Ted operated a cylindrical grinder and he was an outgoing, garrulous cockney who was frequently taunted by his work-mates for being a 'foreigner' and speaking with a funny accent! However, he was greatly respected for his work on behalf of the AEU and he enjoyed lively banter with his engineering colleagues.

Arthur Rogers operated the precision grinder, a highly skilled job. He was a small, studious person who kept very much to himself, but he was extremely competent and knowledgeable

Two Hungarians joined the Toolroom staff in 1956,

following their flight from Hungary to escape the uprising against the Russian occupation of the country. They were Isvan Gal and a turner (lathe operator) known simply as Daz. They were readily accepted by their colleagues and they soon settled into their new surroundings.

An offshoot of the Toolroom was the Tool Repair Section run by charge-hand Sid Turner, a hard-working and very able employee. Two members of this small department that spring to mind are Cliff Bentley, a most affable man, who was also a shop steward and Les Evans a skilled toolmaker.

To indentify the characteristics of the other toolmakers I remember would require a lengthy volume and a prodigious memory, therefore, with apologies to them I am listing the remaining names of those that I had the privilege of working alongside:

John Abbott, D.Atkins, W.Baker, Harold Bartram, Ken Bowles, Len Beaver, D.Bond, Colin Boot, Sam Bradbury, Maurice Campion, Ted Carter, W.Cawthorne, George Cockayne, George Copley, Derek Eden, B.Farnham, Clarence Flowers, M.Foulstone, D.Fox, G.Gaunt, Norman Gunn, A.Haque, J.Hayes, J.Hibbert, D.Hill, C.Hollingsworth, J.Hurst, D.Jackson, Les Jerrom, B.Johnson, D.Knowles, Charlie Limb (Convenor), H.Lupton, Harold Needham, S.Nolan, F.Parsons, A.Pearson, Ted Pettitt, W. Place, A Robinson, Henry Rudge, T.Sikora, M.Smith, A.Taylor, D.Taylor, A.Townsend, J.Wakefield, Sid Whetton, C.Widdison, D.Williams and K.Willis,

The only female operative in the Toolroom was Florence, a stout girl who was very well regarded for her expertise on the band saw. Two other ladies, Sheila Turner and Mrs Hales, worked in the supervisor's office.

One Toolroom operative who cannot be overlooked is Sid Webster, a labourer whose duties included sweeping the floor of the department. Always cheerful, Sid had a wicked habit of creeping up behind you and grabbing the flesh at the back of your thigh. Many an engineer, and particularly an apprentice, can recall the tears his grasp brought to your eyes.

Engineering - Maintenance

This branch of the Engineering department is responsible

for the regular maintenance and repair of plant and machines and also the fitting of guards, feed-chutes and attachments to presses and conveyors.

Frederick Pearson ran this department from 1945 to 1948, when he left to set up in business on his own in the motor trade. He became the owner of a garage on the Doncaster to Nottingham road, near to the White Post Inn, at Farnsfield.

He was succeeded by Frank Smith, a plain-speaking, popular character. Although he was strict with his workforce he nevertheless enjoyed a joke and had many of them played on him. On one occasion Frank boasted to his staff about the new lawn he had just sown. Unbeknown to him some lettuce seeds had been mixed with the lawn seed when Frank had unwittingly left it on his desk. Frank was taken aback when the seed germinated and he had a fine crop of grass and lettuce!

Tall and heavily built, Frank was known to his work-mates as 'Hedgestake Shoulders,' because they sloped at a steep angle. His loud voice could be heard from quite a distance, but he was a fair man with many friends at the factory. He could often be seen walking to work from his home on Croft Avenue, off Robin Down Lane, Mansfield, down Nottingham Road with Jess Farmilo, Jack Slack and Denis Atkins.

Arthur Harris was charge-hand under Frank and he eventually transferred to Sutton-in-Ashfield following the fire there in 1968. A roll call of the Maintenance department includes many unforgettable names. For example, Jack Crowder, who was a very good engineer and always had time for you. Jack was very pleasant to work with and eventually became charge-hand in the department. Ken Else, who spent some time as charge-hand and then supervisor of the department. He was also an accomplished all-round engineer. Ernest Dakin was also a supervisor for a period and he was instrumental in the introduction of a 'planned maintenance' scheme, to fulfil Health and Safety requirements. Keith Hardwick was another charge-hand in the department who carried out his work, particularly on power-presses and inspections, thoroughly and skillfully.

Two characters that I particularly liked were Arthur

Cooke and Alf Downham, old stagers who were very experienced on all types of machines. They enjoyed relating stories of their apprenticeships and never hesitated to help you with any problem that might arise. Arthur and Alf could often be observed walking to and from work in the company of Bill Chamberlain and Jimmy Carlin along Newgate Lane, Mansfield.

Craftsmen like Sammy Coupe were an asset to the department. Sam was responsible for fabricating press guards and complicated metal feed chutes on production lines and presses and he was most precise. A very pleasant, unassuming man, he enjoyed old-time dancing and amateur dramatics, being a member of the Sherwood Dramatic Society and the Mansfield Operatic Society. A great cycling enthusiast, Sam owned a water-cooled Velocette motor cycle at one time. His colleague, Bob Lander was another good sheet metal engineer who, I believe, emigrated to Australia.

Colin Blower, a maintenance engineer, shared some of Sam Coupe's outside interests. Colin possessed a fine tenor voice and was a popular local entertainer. He also performed with the Sherwood Dramatic Society.

Bill Redfern was a general maintenance engineer who enjoyed a drink, during his off-duty hours, in the Redgate public house on Westfield Lane, Mansfield. Bill shared a bench with Brian Day who did similar work, albeit rather slowly, and did not mix with his work-mates. Brian ran a small corner shop on Broxtowe Drive, Mansfield for some years.

An ebullient character, Stan Keeling, was the life and soul of the engineering fraternity, the only man to possess a highly polished bench vice! Some said it was due to his aversion to work, but it was probably a case of sour grapes, for Stan was a gifted engineer who invented many production line modifications. He was also a qualified motor engineer, which made his services much sought after in his non-working time, both by management and fellow workers. A perfect foil to Stan was Harold Thrall, a quiet and conscientious worker.

Another engineer who went about his work without fuss

was George Peck an accomplished, ex-navy engineer who was a devout Christian. He had experienced hardship during the Second World War whilst serving on Arctic convoys. One of George's duties was looking after the factory steam boilers and pumps, a task he performed with precision. George later took on the roll of shop steward, to which he was ideally suited being very sincere and a true gentleman. He was well respected by management for his fairness and his willingness to compromise. George also served on several important committees within the Trade Union movement and received various accolades and honours.

Roy Stubbins, another general maintenance engineer, earned the nickname of 'sleeves,' for you never saw his hands when he was walking through the departments. Brian Day often used to tease him about seeing a stork above his chimney shortly after Roy married a local girl who worked at the factory!

Geoffrey Carlin, who served his apprenticeship with the company, was a delightful person to know and to work with. Geoffrey was very skilled on press maintenance and got on with everyone involved with his work He was a friend of Alfred Armstrong and his bench was next to that of Sid (Lofty) Peach who, along with Cyril Baker, was in the guard-making section. As Sid's nickname suggests he was extremely tall with a deep, resonant voice. He was a bit of a joker and I recall his shouting down the steps to the section working on bulging machine development, 'D-e-e-e-p, S-l-e-e-e-e-p!' as if giving them a wake up call.

Another guard-maker was Douglas Fletcher, who lived on Sheepwalk Lane, Sutton-in-Ashfield and for a time worked at the Sutton factory. He was always telling jokes or trying to wind up his work-mates, but he was extremely good company. He was also very proficient as a guard maker and sheet metal worker.

Stan Clifford was a very able maintenance engineer who was heavily involved in building production machinery and in modifications to plant. A very loyal and sincere person, Stan was a good friend to his fellow workers. William (Bill) Scarlett joined the company from Stokes Castings and was employed mainly on machine pipe work and compressors.

On his retirement he moved to Swindon. Another person who had previously worked at Stokes Castings and had left his post as engineer for the Standard Sand Company to join the Maintenance Department, was Ben Allison. Ben could turn his hand to any problem connected with plant or machinery. In his spare time he ran a small-holding near his home on Somersall Street, Mansfield

An unforgettable character was Roy Allsopp, a great story-teller, who could keep you spellbound. He earned the nickname 'Cowboy,' for he walked with a swagger. A sheet metal worker by trade, Roy left the company, I believe, in the 1970's. Ted Disley, another live wire, joined the department from Rolls Royce, Hucknall. Ted was an astute engineer who worked on numerous projects for production lines, including the bulging process. Ted was one of the recipients of Sid Peach's wake up calls!

Two more engineers I recall who worked in this department were Les Needham and Cyril Dicks. Les was a young engineer engaged on general routine maintenance, who left eventually to join the Education Service as a technician at Sherwood Hall School. Cyril was a lively and outspoken character, married to Edna, who, you will recall later married Noel Fenton.

Two welders formed part of the Maintenance team and one of them, Ernie Donaldson was a plain-speaking Geordie, who reckoned he knew everything. When Ernie was in full cry he could be heard from a great distance, usually giving someone the benefit of his unasked for advice! It was recognised that Ernie was proficient in the larger scale welding tasks, whereas his counterpart, Bernard Witts was a first-class precision welder. Bernard took his job very seriously and could always be relied upon, but he was not averse to a joke and a good gossip, like his pal Cyril Baker. They often enjoyed a natter, especially if there was scandal involved!

The supervisor in charge of the Maintenance Department also had responsibility for the 'Heavy Gang,' a team that required skill in addition to brawn. The team was engaged in the installation, or re-siting of, machines and equipment throughout the factory, under its charge-hand, Ted Parnwell, who had been promoted from the Tool Stores. The strong man of the team was 'Big Charlie' Jennings. I believe he was an ex-rugby player, built like a house side and employees were very careful not to cross him! His team-mates were Frank Whitworth, Len Ashley, Jimmy Carlton, Gus Witts, Harry Sloan, Lionel Grummit and Arthur Williams, father of Scott Williams. These men had a responsible task, for they dealt with the movement of valuable plant, sometimes weighing many tons, guiding it carefully through, or around the departments and securing it to the floor. They always had a skilled maintenance engineer with them whenever precision machinery and heavy presses were being moved.

Frank Whitworth was also responsible for oiling factory machinery not covered by the departments i.e. compressor units and, in the early days, line shafting. Frank was a keen cinema-goer and a great fan of 'The Duke,' cowboy star John Wayne.

Engineering - Electrical Department

This department housed a team of trained electricians initially in the charge of D.Price, an unflappable man, good at his job and well-liked. His successor, Len Fallows, was also an able supervisor and, although not as laid-back as his predecessor, he was popular with his staff.

Len's charge-hand was Bill Brookes who was a good mixer and always eager to hear a joke. Helpful to his work-mates concerning anything electrical, Bill was reliable and down to earth.

In charge later was an exceptional electronics engineer, Brian Crew. During his tenure production machinery was becoming multi-functional and the associated electronics were so sophisticated that Brian spent much of his time designing systems to suit production requirements. He was a superb employee, but sadly, he was forced to retire due to ill health.

Another electrician, George Carter, was employed mainly on shift work together with his labourer Ted Williams. Ted was a comical character and part of his duties was the cleaning of light fittings. Other members of the team were George Bird, who lived at Edwinstowe, Brian

Hardwick, Peter Hopkins, later to become charge-hand, Jim Pogson and Jeff Price, an ex-Royal Navy Petty Officer. The latter was highly strung, which was attributed to his wartime experiences. Nevertheless, Jeff was a very agreeable and sociable person who often enjoyed a drink in the Pheasant public house. These maintenance electricians spent much of their time rewiring machines and plant after re-location.

Frank Warsop, another very able technician, left the trade to pursue a career in politics and was elected Chairman of Nottinghamshire County Council in the 1990's.

Engineering - Apprentices

The company recruited apprentice engineers who were bound by an agreement signed by their respective parents and also by the company management. This document stated that suitable protective clothing must be supplied at the parents' expense and that alehouses were not to be visited by the apprentice!

Apprentices can be divided into two categories - those who joined the company prior to the introduction of the Apprentice Training Centre and those who joined after its inception. In the 1950's came the realisation that skilled engineers were becoming very difficult to recruit on a national basis and that the trend would continue for some time. Through the encouragement of the government sponsored British Productivity Council, the Metal Box Company installed, at most of its factories, apprentice training schemes, which became the envy of many other employers. Two local representatives sat on the Regional Committee of the British Productivity Council and worked towards this end. They were Howard Beadsmore, representing the company and myself, representing the AEU.

The pre-Training Centre apprentices I recall were as follows: Roy Hallam, Roy Perry, Jack Slack, Arnold Mathews, Terry Radford, Ken Nicholson, Selwyn Shaw, Colin Barber, Brian Greenslade, Keith Butler, Alan Plowright, Barry Taylor and David Moss.

Roy Hallam was a good long-distance runner and a member of Meden Valley Harriers. Colin Barber rose through the ranks of British featherweight boxers to be ranked within the top four in the country at that time. He appeared several times on television in various bouts and he was a very quick mover, which he often demonstrated by shadow boxing with his work-mates in the Toolroom. None of them ever picked a real fight with him, I hasten to add!

Selwyn Shaw was a happy go lucky character who was not really cut out for engineering. In one never to be forgotten incident he was a danger to life and limb. Selwyn was operating a horizontal grinder and forgot to switch on the magnetic chuck to secure the base block of the diamond wheel trimmer. Consequently, as soon as the diamond point touched the rotating grinding wheel the block shot from the machine, across a gangway and struck the metal partition of the Inspection Department, producing a severe dent! Luckily no one was in the vicinity at the time. Sadly, Selwyn passed away recently.

David Moss was a talented footballer and cricketer, who eventually became an instructor in the Training Centre.

Several of these apprentices became Toolroom, or Maintenance engineers, and others, like Jack Slack, graduated to the Drawing Office. However, on the first day of their apprenticeship, as raw recruits they would be told all kinds of tales by the seasoned engineers, or asked to go to another department for non-existent tools or equipment. These included such items as a rubber hammer, 'sky hooks,' or a 'long weight!' One unsuspecting novice was sent to the Press Shop for the latter. Having approached the supervisor, Herbert Baggaley and put in his request he was instructed to wait outside Herbert's office. After twenty minutes had elapsed the poor apprentice approached Herbert once more and asked where the 'long weight' was. Herbert replied, 'Well, lad, you've just had it!'

The above-named apprentices served their time in the days of National Service and many of them were called into the forces on completion of their apprenticeship. From memory, the luckiest one was Terry Radford, who was accepted into the Royal Navy, as it was a very difficult service to enter for two years, the standard period served by National Servicemen. Keith Butler served for five years in the Merchant Navy as an alternative to National Service. He was an engineering officer on oil tankers sailing between the United Kingdom and Bahrain.

Many of the apprentices of this era eventually left the company, some after their completion of military service.

In 1954 the Apprentice Training Centre was opened, which gave a superb grounding to potential engineers and there were no limits to how far these young men could progress up the academic ladder. Many apprentices that passed through the Centre qualified as Charted Engineers, by attaining membership of the Institute of Mechanical Engineers.

The teaching staff at the centre was headed by Jack Swift, a Toolroom machinist. He was assisted by Ken Bowles and Tom Foden, both toolmakers. The centre was fully equipped with the appropriate plant and machines and the quality of work produced was very high. Standards of workmanship were established through the module system of the Industrial Training Board and progress was monitored by this body in conjunction with the local Technical College, which ran a day release Mechanical Engineering National Certificate course. The students would spend one day and two evenings at the college in order to pursue National and Higher National Certificate qualifications and, if successful, go on to degree courses, or M. I. Mech. E. qualifications.

Competitions were held for the award of Apprentice of the Year, which encouraged a high class of workmanship and produced many first-class engineers who were guaranteed employment with the company. All the students were members of the AEU, which also monitored their training programme by means of the monthly Engineering Sub-Committee meetings held at the factory. Following the annual Metal Box Company trade test for apprentices, in 1956, one of the apprentices, Barry Skinner was selected to represent the United Kingdom at an international competition in Madrid. He won first prize in the milling section, a great tribute to Barry's skill and training.

It is interesting to note that in the Training Centre's first year, only four bound apprentices were appointed. These were Edgar Greasley, Peter Hudson, Terry Parsons and Brian

Baxter. They soon fitted into the new regime, which would continue for approximately twenty years.

The second year intake was much larger, the scheme having bedded in. This comprised Derek Wilson, Fred Wood, Roy Lunn, Arthur Davies, Ivan Kingswood, Barry Clarke, Stuart Bramwell and Tony Bloxam.

Third year apprentices were Michael Pye, David Hawkins, Brian Shaw, Keith Skermer, Donald Blagg, Keith Dunston, R.Parker and B.Draycott.

A regular annual intake of eight apprentices had been established and the fourth year apprentices were Ernest Dakin, K.Peat, K.Nicholson, Alf Powell, P.Whitlam, Tony Hinchcliffe, Brian Gent and D.Johnson. Tony Hinchcliffe played drums with a local group, known as Shane Fenton and the Fentones. Shane Fenton later changed his name to Alvin Stardust and rose to stardom.

It is pertinent to mention that the training of these apprentices included visits to factories and places of interest, which even included the local Empire Cinema. A thriving series of social activities was also in being and was run under the umbrella of the factory Sports and Social Club. The Metal Box Adventure Club was instigated in 1955 by a group of apprentices. It had its own badge and followed the spirit of the Outward Bound Schools and White Hall, a centre for country pursuits at Buxton in Derbyshire. The club became self-supporting through dances and social functions that helped to raise funds for hill-walking, climbing and pot-holing equipment. Brian Gent, an eighteen -year-old apprentice was appointed a pot-holing instructor on weekend courses at White Hall, a great honour for the club. The most important feature of this club was the teamwork that it generated.

Sadly, in the 1970's the Training Centre was closed on economic grounds and future training reverted, more or less, to that in the years before its inception. Apprentice training was also reduced on a national basis, which, I believe, was a short-sighted move that caused skill shortages within the engineering industry for decades afterwards.

When the Centre closed Tom Foden was appointed Factory Health and Safety Officer, due to his being a member of the St. John's Ambulance Brigade. Tom made a firm success of the job and later he combined the position with that of Head of Factory Security. Jack Swift suffered ill health and died after a short illness. He was a great loss to the company, a most sincere man who was proud of his achievements and those of the apprentices under his guidance. Ken Bowles left the company to become a publican at North Hykeham, Lincolnshire, after a spell as manager at the Queen Victoria public house in Mansfield.

I wonder where the fore-mentioned apprentices are today? I should also indicate the names of those apprentices that joined the company at a later date. They are J.Kelsall, Jed Hurst, Jeff Carlin, Shaun Nolan, Chris Nolan, Nigel Crapper, David Clayton, David Feally, Robert Crowder, John Thrall, Edward Charles, Andy Evans, Peter Hurt, Michael Bonser, Luegi Incerti, Paul Halfpenny, B.Speed, Richard Needham, Alan Stocks, Brian Alvey and A.Butler. Richard Needham won a National Award for constructing a tinplate model of a windmill.

Engineering - Drawing Office

This department was staffed mainly by apprentice-trained engineers holding engineering qualifications and, by engineers with Toolroom experience. One memorable draughtsman, George Stevens, who was nearing retirement, could frequently be discovered enjoying a nap in the afternoons. He was safely hidden from the Chief Draughtsman's view by the surrounding drawing boards!

Jack Slack was Senior Draughtsman for a period and he was followed, as far as I can recall, by Ralph Downham, Bert Moakes, Jess Farmilo and Derek Wilson. The draughtsmen I recollect were Peter Barsby, S.Lowe, Brian Valentine, L.Hudson, Paul Foulkes, Ron Gwillam, D.Patterson and Roy Lunn. Brian Longstaff was Senior Planning and Development Engineer based in the Drawing Office. Several of the above progressed further within the company, such as Bert Moakes, who eventually became Works Manager.

Three ladies worked in the department as tracers, one of who, Doreen Bradley was married to Harry Bradley who worked in the Toolroom at Mansfield prior to becoming charge-hand in the Toolroom at Sutton-in-Ashfield.

Work Study

In the 1950's the new innovation of 'Time and Motion Study' was establishing itself in this country. The instigator of its introduction to the company was Tom Peacock, the man responsible for producing one of the manuscripts upon which this book is based. Tom performed a variety of jobs over the years. He was a good organiser and a sociable character who married Miss Jenner. She ran a small poultry farm on Derby Road, Mansfield and, for a period lodged with my parents who lived on the same road. Tom is remembered most for forming the Work Study team that was created to improve production techniques and efficiency in all departments. The Metal Box Company at that time was keen to install this system on a national scale and Tom spent a considerable time in America studying improvements in production methods. On his return this new department soon became a focus of attention. Various studies were conducted on production lines, including photo studies of many operations that were reproduced in slide form and used for demonstration and training purposes. Tom eventually visited other branches of the Metal Box Company to give lectures on the techniques employed. He was assisted by Ernest Wincup and later by an engineer whose name, I believe, was Richard Parker. Alan Gosling, a company trainee in the engineering estimating section was later added to the team. The sad outcome, once the department was well-established, was that Tom and Ernest left the company to join the Ann Shaw Organisation, which was a leading force in the country regarding the development of Work Study techniques.

In the early 1960's Pat Barrett was appointed to the position of Work Study Officer. A very go-ahead person, Pat was soon offered the position of Factory Manager with the Metal Box Company (Overseas Division). He was sent abroad to oversee the building of a completely new factory in Chittagong, lying in the Bay of Bengal, an area notorious for typhoons and massive tidal waves. When the factory was two-thirds complete it was flattened by a typhoon! Knowing Pat and the man he was, I'll wager he had the factory re-built in record time!

The Work Study Officers that followed Pat Barrett were Michael Horton, Alan Plowright and Michael Smith.

Factory Services - Joinery and Plumbing

The joiner's shop was run by Harold Sansom who lived on Sandhurst Avenue, Mansfield, in a bungalow that he helped to build. On his retirement Fred Rudge, brother of Henry Rudge, a Toolroom engineer, took over the helm. Fred was a very pleasant and obliging man, who was only too willing to offer advice concerning wood-working and DIY.

Under their control were good craftsmen, such as George Kimberley, E.Paling, Fred Winter and later, Ray Ward. In addition to routine factory maintenance they made packing tables, press tables and packing jigs for use on production lines. Also manufactured were packing cases for transportation of goods and seaming machine 'distance blocks,' which had to be accurately shaped.

A labourer in the department was Jim Turley, whose job became redundant and he was offered a position in the Boiler House.

Below the joiner's shop in the factory yard was the plumber's shop run by Stan Hodgkin and later by Don Osbourne. Stan was very knowledgeable about his trade and always helpful.

Factory Services - Boiler House

In the early days the Boiler House was situated beneath the Factory Manager's office, a rather precarious state of affairs! One can imagine the noise and vibration that was generated, not to mention the risk of explosion. Eventually wisdom prevailed and the Boiler House was moved to an area known by the employees as 'Sparrow Park,' a pleasant small garden with seats, opposite the factory. I remember the Boiler House staff at that time as Jim Turley, (mentioned above) an ex-Royal Navy Stoker, W.H.Bailey and Andy Dunlop.

Tool-Setting

Many of the tool-setters working in the various production departments have been identified under the staffing of those departments. However, one person who deserves particular mention is Harold Simpson, who followed Alfred Armstrong as Mayor of Mansfield, in 1958. When Councillor Simpson took office, aged thirty-nine, he was introduced in local newspaper headlines as 'The Youngest Mayor Ever.' Harold was born on Christmas Day in Bould Street, Mansfield. Educated at King Edward School he began his working life at fourteen on the staff of the Co-operative Dairy, before joining the company in 1955. During the Second World War he served in the RAF and spent two and a half years in Southern Rhodesia (now Zimbabwe). In November 1946, a few weeks after his demobilisation, he was elected to the Borough Council and remained a Councillor for the East Ward until 1965. Harold met his wife-to-be, Gladys, when they were both young members of the Labour Party and they were married in 1945. Gladys is the daughter of the late Agnes Milford, who was Mayor in 1956 and she had the unique distinction of being Mayoress to both her mother and her husband.

In his younger days, before the Second World War, Harold enjoyed swimming and became captain of the Co-operative Water Polo Team. He had a great interest in painting, being an amateur artist. One of the most enjoyable events of his mayoral year was opening the annual exhibition of the Mansfield Society of Artists. He was privileged to be chosen as Chairman of the Nottingham panel of judges in the BBC contest 'Top Town.' Harold was a very reliable member of the Sherwood Dramatic Society for over thirty years, fifteen of those performing the duties of Property Manager. He also took an active part in the proceedings when the Palace Theatre was purchased by the Council and became the Civic Hall, and later the Civic Theatre, before reverting to its original name.

Harold left the company in the 1960's to join the Water Board, eventually becoming Chief Store Keeper. Taking early retirement he continued his involvement with the local community as a member of several organisations and committees.

Tool Stores

For some years this was in the care of Bert Worthington who distributed the relevant sets of tooling to the production departments and the Toolroom, as and when required.

Tinplate and Carton Stores

Under the floor of the Press Shop was sited the Tinplate Store, Goods In section and the cardboard carton storage area known as the 'Rat Hole.' In charge was Bill Rose assisted by charge-hand Clemence (Clem) Gundel. Harry Radford was the carton storeman and Sam Wakeling and Gus Witts were operatives in the Tinplate Store. Gus Witts operated the tinplate-waxing machine for approximately fifteen years before joining the Slitting Department. At one time, as has been mentioned, Gus was a member of the 'Heavy Gang.' Later John Truman took over as supervisor. Two girls worked in the department office, namely Freda Gant and Joan Morrell.

Sample Room

A small room in the factory, vital to the Commercial Department, is the Sample Room, stocked with samples of tins and other items produced since the company's early years. However, some samples have disappeared, which has hindered the piecing together of product history. The most damaging occurrence in this respect was during the 1970's when the order was given to destroy all samples of toys produced in the Mansfield and Sutton-in-Ashfield factories. This decision wiped out at a stroke the complete toy-making legacy and, during the centenary celebrations of the company, in 1995, appeals were made to the public for toys that had been produced at the two factories. The response was poor and a mere four samples were offered, with no clockwork toys included.

At the time when the toy samples were destroyed employees were not allowed to purchase them. Tool-setters were employed on several Saturday mornings to (in Cyril

The men in White Coats!
~raughtsmen Derek Wilson, Roy Hallam and Colin Lesson, in 1960

Parents Evening held in the Mansfield Factory canteen, in 1957

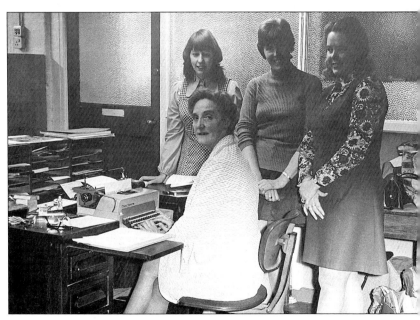

Miss Brooks and 'Girls', in the 1970s

Press Shop Tool-setters, in the 1950's

Retirement Presentation to Hilda Scothern by Jack Selby,
in the early 1960's

Long Service Award Presentation, in 1980

Retirement Presentation to Maud Kershaw, in 1957

Long Service Award Presentation, in 1977

Edith Clarke's Retirement, in 1960

Long Service Award Presentation, in the early 1960's

Long Service Award Presentation, in 1964

Long Service Award Presentation by Sir Robert Barlow, in 1964

Long Service Award Presentation by C. W. Parkinson, in 1974

Long Service Award Presentation, around 1970

Aerial view of the Mansfield Factory as it is today

Repton's words) 'destroy our heritage by smashing them to pieces with hammers and scrapping them.' One can appreciate that Health and Safety regulations concerning toys were due to come into force, but some could have been retained for presentation in the Exhibition Gallery and others sold to adult collectors only. None of them need have fallen into children's hands.

The Sample Room was ably run by Winnie Slack and then by Vera Musson, who lived on Haddon Road, Mansfield and died in 1999 after an extensive retirement. Vera, a religious person, was very strict concerning the issue of samples and she ran the department with great efficiency. She knew where every sample item was stored and how many were in stock, which was important in ensuring that stocks were never completely depleted.

Vera also dealt with the parcel post, sending samples to potential customers and dealing with returned samples arriving by post. She was loyal and hard working and, on her retirement she was replaced by Joyce Bryan, who transferred from the Talcum Department. Joyce learnt the ropes very quickly and took a leaf from Vera's book when it came to the number of samples anyone was allowed to take from the store. Like Vera she was very conscientious and loyal to the company, also attending all the departmental parties, where she was fun to be around. Joyce has written a short article describing life during the Second World War (See Appendix 9) that appears in the publication by the Old Mansfield Society entitled 'Mansfield in the War Years.' At the present time, Joyce serves on the Pensioners' Committee.

When Joyce retired her successor was Joan Evans, who had previously worked in Seamless Department, giving many years of loyal service there. Joan is a well-known member of the St John's Ambulance Brigade, holding a Superintendent's post at Glapwell. A very hard worker, she was responsible for ably re-stocking the new Exhibition Gallery.

Gatehouse/Commissionaire

In the early 1900's the post of Commissionaire was held by Frank Maxted. Later, the aforementioned Charlie Kilminster took over the position and also control of the gatehouse, assisted by Jack Reece, Lou Truscott, A.Brewin and Ken Dennison. During World War Two it was used as a home guard post and concrete bunkers were constructed around the factory perimeter for look out purposes and were used by the Home Guard battalion, consisting of company personnel.

Production Control

It has been indicated that Eddie Walsh took over this department after the Second World War, before he was promoted to Factory Manager. He was assisted by Fred Renshaw, a small person who could be seen first thing each morning making his rounds of the factory production offices, clipboard in hand. Fred gave the impression of carrying the entire weight of factory production on his shoulders, for he was always hurrying and wearing a harassed expression.

Eddie Walsh was followed as Production Controller by Peter McCracken, a well-educated and competent manager. Later, Brian Hall took over the position, having transferred from Sutton-in-Ashfield. Brian, a tall, imposing character had lots of confidence and applied himself energetically to his task. He ran an efficient department, which included female staff and also ex-Production Supervisors, namely, Herbert Baggaley and Sid Clarke, in advisory positions.

Much has been written about Herbert, but Sid deserves a mention for his conscientious and loyal service to the company in various capacities and for his prowess as a cricketer. He played for the Mansfield Racecourse and latterly for the Mansfield Metal Box team. Whilst batting during one unforgettable match for the factory team, Sid scored one of the fastest centuries ever seen in local league cricket. He also had the dubious distinction of pole-axing two umpires at the start of a match on the Oddicroft Lane ground! Sid was having a practice batting session near the pavilion as the umpires emerged from it to begin proceedings. Sid received a tempting slow ball from his practice partner and promptly struck it hard. Unfortunately, with superb timing, he managed to graze the back of the head of the nearest umpire, who promptly fell on his face through shock. The second umpire was struck on the temple and fell backwards. Sid's face was a picture as he surveyed the scene of carnage and he ran desperately to the inert umpires to ascertain the damage. Remarkably, after several minutes they had recovered sufficiently to start the match and unsurprisingly the factory team was the victim of several harsh decisions by the sore-headed umpires!

Artists' Department

The artists were eventually moved into new studios, which were excellent and resembled a holy sanctuary. Oak-panelled walls and cubicles added taste, as did the alabaster statues and miniature palm trees. Whilst the artists were in residence, it is said, you could hear a pin drop.

Later, the department was altered again and staff numbers were increased. All the artists became full time employees with pension rights and other benefits. The staff I recall at that time was Len Tooke, Studio Manager, Edgar Allcock, Steve Radford, Ernest Marsh, E.Payne, E.Ward, A.Bruin and Keith Creswell, an artist with a passion for paintings of steam trains. Captain Parker was the librarian responsible for design literature and period artwork. He inherited the library from Tom Peacock, who played a major roll in its formation.

Edgar Allcock, who was also a magician and a member of the Magic Circle, took over as Studio Manager when Len Tooke retired. Edgar was followed by Steve Radford, a very talented artist, who painted many notable local buildings and scenes of Mansfield.

Commercial

Maurice Boaler was deputy to L.J.Wass in the early days and he eventually left the company to join the Barnsley Tin Box and Canister Company. I am sure his presence was missed, for he was very able and popular with his colleagues.

Bob Knight ran the department after the war until he was succeeded by J.G.Young who had worked first at Carlisle and then Metal Box India. Ill-health necessitated George taking the less stressful post of Buying Office Manager. A member of his staff in Commercial was Jim Wass, a flamboyant character, totally different to his father, but a very competent and successful salesman. He had the honour of having his photograph printed on a book-shaped container manufactured for Bassett's Confectionery and designed to hold photographs when it had been emptied of sweets.

Ralph Gutteridge spent a period in the department following his demobilisation from the forces. I understand Ralph also spent time at the Sutton-in-Ashfield factory and worked with Edith Hart and Roland Barrington in a small Commercial office. Ralph was eventually promoted to the post of Manager of the Alperton factory.

Colin Henshaw, I believe, was followed by John Scott, a very able salesman, who pursued business abroad, mainly in the USA. One company in particular, Imported Delicacies, was a very good customer that he built up a relationship with. John was an accomplished musician in his free time and he had his own dance band, which played at a number of social functions at the factory. He retired early from the company to concentrate on his musical career.

Ralph Stone was responsible for the Worcester Ware section of the business and Norman Candy, assisted by Valerie Marshall, handled the commercial side of the Extrusion Department. John Manning was mainly concerned with the marketing of biscuit tins.

Other male Commercial staff included Len Patrick, Arthur Annabel and Mike Tindall.

On the female side were Molly Allcock, Florence Rossiter, who was replaced by Margaret Cresswell and Rita Page, who, unfortunately had to retire early through ill health. Other ladies included Sandra Rogers, Kay Webster, Pam Dent (Green), Barbara Plowright (Hulme) and Carol Truman, who married John Abbott, a Toolroom engineer. Ann Stockdale began as an Office Junior and eventually became a very able Commercial staff member. Ann was eventually promoted to the post of Personnel Officer and she remained as such until her retirement. She is now secretary of the Pensioners' Association.

I believe that Sue Briggs, who worked in the department, is still with the company.

Estimating/Standard Costs

Post-war members of this department were Charlie Scott, Harry Allsopp, who later became Office Manager in the 1950's, Arthur Littlewood (Junior), J.O.Walker, David Charlton and Ted Brooks, who was married to Marlene in the Wages Department.

Arthur Littlewood was a good sportsman who particularly enjoyed tennis and he played a major roll on the Sports and Social Committee for many years.

The ladies I recall were Eileen Guilor, Max Melling, Margaret Kitchen and Miss Quible.

Buying

Sid Bills ran the department for a number of years following the Second World War. Dawson Collins, whose father worked in the Artists' Department, assisted J.G.Young during his term in charge and he eventually took over the department. Dawson had a keen memory and was always willing to assist with any problems regarding supply of components. If a specialist supplier was necessary Dawson was the man to find one and, in that respect he was invaluable.

Joan Bull moved from Sutton-in-Ashfield and eventually took control of Buying. Soon afterwards all the staff that knew her were very pleased to hear the announcement of her forthcoming marriage. Like Ann Stockdale, Joan, whose married name is Abbott, is now a valued and very active committee member of the Pensioners' Association

Support staff in the department were Chris Hatton, Miss Valentine, Miss Trotter and Jean Brown who married Denis Atkins.

Accounts

The head of this department in the 1950's/1960's was Bertram (Bert) Meadows a reserved, but highly regarded and valuable member of the management team. Tragically, he lost his wife, a bitter blow to him and some years later he married a friend of many years standing, known to all as Dorothy Ford. She was Office Manager when they married and they had a happy life together. Dorothy died in her eighties, in April 1998.

Assisting Bert Meadows was Derek Barker, who eventually transferred to Sutton-in-Ashfield as Head of Accounts. Derek suffered ill health for some time and he passed away on January 1st 2000. Roy Gill was also working in the department during Bert's tenure.

David Petch took over the department on Bert's retirement, but he was also obliged to leave the company for health reasons, although still in his prime. He was well remembered for his helpfulness and extensive knowledge.

Wages/Cashier

In earlier years the Chief Cashier was Sidney Slack (Senior), who was followed by his son Sidney. Sidney (Junior) was a lively and entertaining character who was popular with his fellow employees and remained a bachelor. He was a member of the Mansfield Operatic Society and performed many leading roles with great expertise.

Derek Brown, a very accomplished accountant, succeeded Sidney (Junior) and later he transferred to Sutton-in-Ashfield, from where he retired. Derek was very involved in charity work, particularly in providing help for the disabled in Mansfield.

Winnie Marriott then joined the company from the Mansfield Building Society as Chief Cashier. A very amenable and sociable person, Winnie had a good sense of humour and attended all the factory social events, being a keen member of the Sports and Social Club. She was difficult to replace on her retirement.

However, a suitable person was found, namely Betty Ellis who possessed a similar personality to her predecessor and was equally active in the social field. Betty was extremely helpful with any wage or tax query and she is presently treasurer of the Pensioners' Association.

It is regrettable that the staff underwent many changes and, unfortunately, my memory of other members of this department is very scant.

General Manager's Office

All the General Managers were supported by dedicated

clerical staff and private secretaries. Nora Witham followed Miss Gutteridge as private secretary and she was succeeded in turn by Nora Beckett, very trustworthy, trained to the highest standards and extremely loyal to her employers. Nora was followed by Ondrey Allsopp, a charming person and a very efficient secretary, probably due to her excellent filing system. Jean Teare succeeded Ondrey and I am sure she inherited all the qualities of her predecessors. Jean was particularly loyal, well respected and always pleased to help anyone. I found her very courteous and a true private secretary.

In addition to the above there was a full back-up service supplied by the Personnel Department.

General Office

The department known as General Office overlapped many of the previous office functions and unfortunately I am unable to recall accurately where some of the staff were deployed. I believe Chris Kinghorn was Office Manager for a time, but, with apologies, I am listing others concerned, without their location:

Arthur Lloyd Birks (mentioned previously), Bill Goodman, Norman Ely, plus, of course, the ladies, Molly Alcock, Florence Healey, Ada Morgan, Joan Blagg (Shepherd), Julie Lunn (Presgrave) and Vivienne Wass.

Personnel

An important innovation within the Metal Box Company was the establishment of Factory Personnel Departments. This was a big advance on the old system whereby the Factory Manager would be the person to offer employment, (so ably indicated by Eddie Walsh in his contribution). Employee records were put onto a database and their progress monitored. In addition to a contract of employment, employees received a copy of the company's Works Committee Charter and a medical carried out by the company doctor.

Prior to the introduction of the above system, the department was known as the Welfare Department and two of its members at that time were Miss Barrington and Miss

Cissie Massey.

Under the new regime the first Personnel Officer was Albert Wilson who had replaced John Stewart. I believe he had occupied a similar position in the army and was ideally suited to the roll. Albert was courteous, compassionate and genuine. He knew the workings of the company, was very approachable and a good organiser. Albert was eventually promoted to Extrusion Manager at Sutton-in-Ashfield, a position from which he retired and moved home to Matlock.

Albert's replacement was William (Bill) Dickie, a Carlisle man who was very experienced in industrial law and procedures, a vital requirement for the post. At the outset Bill was not easy to get on with, but as I got to know him I found him fair in his dealings and very approachable. Regarding any matters that affected working relations between management and the unions, his door was always open from 8am until 8-30am each morning for an unofficial chat. Many problems were solved in this manner, which saved time and money. Whenever I met Bill outside of work we always enjoyed a chat and although we had many battles at work, mutual respect and compromise was the key to our good relations. Bill died on May 1st 2000, aged ninety-four.

When Bill retired he was succeeded by W.Wileman for a short time. John Watts then took over, a man who had served in East Africa, as a Captain with the East African Rifles, before joining the Metal Box Company (Overseas Division). A very different character from his predecessors, John was very polite and quietly spoken. He seemed to find working in an English industrial environment very different to his army career, but he coped very well and soon learnt the 'nitty gritty' of industrial relations. I believe that John delegated much work to his subordinates as he was a laid back person who appeared to have few worries. Nevertheless he was popular and commanded respect and he played a major roll in persuading the company pensioners to set up a committee to co-ordinate their activities. When he retired he was not replaced due to reorganisation of the department and a reduction in its staff. John remains a bachelor and I have seen him occasionally since his retirement and enjoyed a chat.

On the female side of personnel management I recall Miss W.L.Allsopp, who was in the same class (metaphorically) as Albert Wilson. An extremely nice person to talk to, she was a very good counsellor for the factory girls and well thought of by them. Miss Allsopp was an understanding person who tried her best to solve any problems encountered by her 'girls.' It was a sad loss when she left to take a post closer to her home near Sheffield.

Sheila Hunt took over as Personnel Officer for a time before she left the company to run a successful business. She was a highly effective manager, held in high esteem by all the factory employees.

The last female Personnel Officer was Ann Stockdale, who, you will recall worked in Commercial prior to her appointment. Ann was very competent and ran an efficient department. She was still in the post when it became that of Personnel Manager and she retired from the company when the department was reduced and re-named Human Resources.

The position of Assistant Personnel Officer was filled by the following during my time with the company:

Mr Posser who, I believe, assisted John Watts. He was transferred, after a short period, to the Palmers Green factory as Personnel Officer.

Mr E.Jackson, who like Mr Posser did not stay long and left the company.

Assistant to Miss Allsop was Jean Bartholomew.

Clerical staff in the department that I recall are Margaret Parkin, D.Riddell, Joan Philips, Kath Burton, (Later to join the Buying Department) Jill Clay, Marlene Overton, Glenys Kingswood and Rae McGee.

During the tenure of Bill Dickie, Angus Keillor joined the team as a trainee Personnel Officer before transferring to the Hull factory. I believe he returned to the Sutton-in-Ashfield factory for a period and now runs his own business in Newark.

Personnel/ Medical Centre

There was a close link between the Personnel Department and the Medical Centre. The former provided assistance in addressing any personal problems, for there was always a male or female Personnel Officer to confide in. In addition to administering first aid, the latter was a place where sound medical advice could be sought and any follow up treatment recommended by a doctor would be dealt with. Certain inoculations were also given, but most importantly cancer screening for women and hearing tests were carried out and monitored by expert staff. One could even purchase cod liver oil capsules at a discount. Sadly, many of these admirable facilities no longer exist and the centre is only manned part-time.

The above services ensured a good relationship between the company and its employees. If the company wished to complain about an employee, a procedure was in place to deal with such an occurrence. In these cases the applicable trade union would be involved in discussions, from a Health and Safety and discipline aspect.

From 1939 onwards the Personnel Department embraced a welcome amenity for employees by arranging visits to holiday and convalescent homes, operated on behalf of the Metal Box Company's benevolent fund by a small committee at the Hull branch. The homes were sited in Hornsea, Bournemouth and at Gretna, in Scotland.

The benevolent fund was presented with Mascotte House at Hornsea in Yorkshire by Mr J.Crabtree. Those at Bournemouth, namely Sutton House and Hepworth House were given by Mr Ernest Barlow. Dormy House at Gretna was very popular, but little is known of its history. I understand there was also a holiday home in Torquay for use by senior management.

The Personnel Department was also responsible for arranging summer outings for the company's pensioners. Allowances for meals were provided and one of the outings was free of charge. Each year a Christmas party was held for the pensioners with entertainment and a present provided. This was greatly appreciated, as was the company Christmas parcel, containing a good selection of food for the festive season. All the items were packed in Metal Box Company containers, be it tin or cardboard and the parcels distributed by the Personnel Department.

At present, company involvement in these amenities is financial support for an annual outing and sponsorship for special events. In 2000, the company pensioners received support for a party to celebrate the Millennium and it is good to find that past employees, who helped to make the Metal Box Company a leading force in precision engineering and food and commodity packaging, have not been forgotten.

The Medical Centre has had several sites during its history and, after the Second World War it was housed in the factory yard in a building originally built as a decontamination centre as part of wartime air raid precautions.

The dedicated staff included a hospital-trained Nursing Sister assisted by qualified nursing staff. In the early years Miss Boyes ran the centre and she was followed by Sister Young who was in charge during the 1950's. She was a splendid 'medic' who mothered the employees and she performed very minor operations and stitched severe cuts in addition to carrying out normal first aid. I remember her possibly saving Ron Gwillam's life after a horrific accident. Ron was a Departmental Engineer at the time and was given a job, after his recovery, in the Drawing Office. Whilst working on a tool in a press his hand was partially severed when it operated without warning. Sister Young applied a tourniquet to his arm and bandaged his wound immediately, after summoning an ambulance. She lived in Hucknall and enjoyed a long retirement.

Amongst the support staff was a small, chatty lady, Mrs Cummings, who put everyone at ease and treated them kindly. Two others I recall are Ethell Reece and Miss Naylor. Ethell was very pleasant, but a bit of a scandal monger, so she was able to take your mind off your injury. Miss Naylor, I believe, eventually transferred to the National Health Service.

Canteen

This was referred to at one time as 'Arcadia Hall,' Its name probably originated during the period when the factory was known as 'Arcadia Works.' It was really the social hub of the factory and, being subsidised by the company, provided a good service. During the Second World War the canteen was used for briefing employees and, despite a food shortage, received an allowance to assist in providing meals of reasonable quality. I should mention that a wartime canteen, called The British Restaurant, was available to all workers of the district for a mid-day meal. It was on the site of the Queen's Cinema, later used for ballroom dancing. Meals cost fivepence (2P) for main meal plus sweet. Soup and bread roll cost an extra tuppence (under 1P). The selection of food was very good and nicely cooked.

The canteen staff was always obliging and the canteen managers I recall are Mrs Ellrick, Mr Smithers, George Wilde, T.Healey, Mrs Wooley, Eva Shaw, Miss S.Hunt and Mavis Marriott.

Sybil Harrison and Evelyn Caddy were excellent pastry cooks, particularly Sybil, who joined the canteen staff from Harvey's (Bakers) of Cavendish Street, Mansfield.

Today the canteen serves basic meals only and most drinks are dispensed from machines. There is no longer a trolley service to all departments in the factory that was formerly provided by canteen staff, such as Nan Stewart, who served hot and cold drinks, biscuits and cakes.

Sutton-in-Ashfield - Printing

Following the transfer of printing to Sutton-in-Ashfield, I remember the printers of that period as George Candy, (Norman Candy's father) who was foreman, assisted by Norman Armstrong, Tommy Allen, George Tipping and Alan Horsefield (son of Jack Horsefield).

W.Ormston, Printing Manager, retired in 1963 and he was replaced by T.Allsop and eventually by Wilf Bonsall. Other supervisory staff in the department during the 1960's were Stan Walker (Supervisor), Keith Piercy (Foreman), Oswald Stordy (Foreman and brother of Howard Stordy) and J.Golding (Reproduction Supervisor)

Sutton-in-Ashfield - Production Control

David Whitlam is a person I recall in addition to other

Controllers, who have been mentioned previously as having spent periods at Sutton.

Sutton-in-Ashfield - Engineering/Product Design

Two outstanding engineers come to mind, namely Seth Fortune and Arthur Dove. Seth was Toolroom Foreman and Arthur (his son-in-law) became involved in product design. Both men were great designers and innovators, particularly in the field of toys. They did ground breaking work on Burnett and Chad Valley Toys and 'U-Builda' toy kits. As previously mentioned they also developed the bulging process.

Arthur was an accomplished director of amateur stage productions, which included the annual children's Christmas pantomime, held in the Sutton factory canteen. He also liked motoring and visiting his bungalow at Sutton-on-Sea in Lincolnshire. Arthur was an exceptional character and it is unfortunate that he did not enjoy good health during his short retirement.

A little later, E.Ellis joined the Product Design section from the Raleigh Cycle Company, of Nottingham and he was mainly concerned with design of containers and advertising products, such as display tablets.

When part of the General Line production at Sutton was transferred to Mansfield, the following staff also relocated. Oswald Bacon, Arthur Dove, Graham Becket, Warner Pitchford, Tommy Jewsbury, Bill Speed and William Allen.

Oswald Bacon vacated the post of Toolroom Foreman to return to Mansfield and he joined the engineering estimating section working alongside Ernest Fletcher, Noel Fenton and Alan Gosling. Alan eventually transferred to Head Office to become a member of the Work Study team.

Graham Beckett replaced Oswald Bacon and he was later to return to Mansfield and join the engineering estimating section. Graham will be remembered for his stalwart service to the AEU as branch treasurer and as a very reliable and sincere person.

Over the years the Sutton Toolroom had its share of skilled engineers and unforgettable characters, one of the most memorable being Fred Wilkes. A good toolmaker, Fred always sported a flat cap, even when working and usually had a cigarette dangling from the corner of his mouth. You always knew when he was around, for he was continually imitating the sound of brass instruments. He was a talented musician and, in addition to his membership of the Kirkby Colliery Brass Band, Fred conducted the band that accompanied the annual children's Christmas pantomime.

Another performer in the pantomime was Tommy Jewsbury, who, like Bill Speed and Ted Lewis worked for a time with Arthur Dove on product design and model-making. All these engineers, including Arthur Dove were eventually transferred to Mansfield, along with Newman Gunn. Arthur was confined to the Artists' Department and limited to Product Design and the remainder entered a large Toolroom environment, which at that time was under the supervision of Howard Stordy. Model-making came under Howard's control and I joined a small enclave, designing and making models, together with Tommy Jewsbury. Unfortunately, Tommy never got on with Howard Stordy and asked to be transferred back to Sutton. After trade union intervention, this was agreed, but sadly, the strain of the upheaval weighed heavily upon him

Another character from the same era as Fred Wilkes was Arthur 'Snuffy' Smith, a cheerful man who had a perpetual brown stain above his upper lip caused by the regular inhaling of snuff. His loud sneezes after inhaling would invariably startle his Toolroom colleagues.

Amongst other Toolroom staff was Arthur Richardson, who left to join a rival packaging company, Illingworths, also of Sutton-in-Ashfield.

Harry Bradley, who was transferred from Mansfield to become charge-hand, was a musician who played the euphonium in a local band. Like Fred Wilkes, Harry would frequently imitate the sounds of brass, so the Toolroom was a very tuneful place!

Other engineers included Maurice Smith, a reserved and sincere person, Rex Day, a popular, out-going character and Basil Sugg, a very skilled toolmaker. Sid Smith transferred to Mansfield and took charge of the 9¼ Biscuit and

Margarine Tin production line. Sid, a very amenable man, lived on Bathwood Drive, Sutton-in-Ashfield.

The Sutton factory had a small, but very effective maintenance department, several of whose members transferred to Mansfield. These were Lawrence Dillon Arthur Harris and Maurice Hunt. Arthur Harris joined the company from Stokes Castings and he ran the department whilst at Sutton with a quiet, but pleasant demeanour, which made him popular with his staff. Maurice Hunt was a skilled engineer, particularly experienced on printing machines. Later, Graham Simpson, another maintenance engineer, moved in the reverse direction by transferring from Mansfield to Sutton, from where he retired.

Other engineering staff at Sutton in the 1950's and onwards were: A.Audsley, C.Patrick, R.Cox, B.Leatherland, S.Hoare, M.Dillon, M.Hunt, R.Gillott (electrician), A.Newby, G.Asher, G.Morgan, B.Handley, B.Oxby, J.Gregory, N.Scott and P.Bloom.

General Line Production - Sutton- in-Ashfield

In 1962, at the time of the transfer of part of the above production, Alfred (Alf) Hill (Supervisor) and his forewoman, Rose Draycott moved to Mansfield. Alf was a cheerful character, well liked by the production staff, for he always ready for a laugh and a joke. However, I saw the other side of Alf as a caring individual who was very concerned about the well being of company pensioners. Without fail he would contact them regularly to inquire if they needed assistance and do all he could to help them. Alf passed away in 1999 whilst in his eighties. Rose became forewoman in the Press Shop at Mansfield.

Taking over from Alf Hill at Mansfield was Edward (Eddie) Temple, a time-served engineer who worked within the Metal Box Company (Overseas Division) at Dar-es-Salam, in East Africa. A very able craftsman, Eddie was employed on machine development initially before moving into departmental management. I found Eddie a straight-talker, who did not mince his words. If you got on with him you were his friend for life and he enjoyed partnering Scott Williams, Harry Bradley and Jack Tyler for frequent rounds of golf at the Coxmoor course. His passion was restoring Classic cars and on his retirement he was able to indulge his hobby.

Sutton-in-Ashfield – General

The transfer of production from Mansfield to Sutton from the 1940's onwards involved Printing, Extrusion and Worcester Ware departments. The following members of staff, who have not been mentioned previously, were employed during this period. Print Managers, A.N.Kent and C.Banner. Platemaking, R.Round, S.King, T.Crabtree. Print supervisors, F.Bull and later Gordon Beastall, who joined the Company in the 1950's. Gordon spent a period with Metal Box (Overseas Division) before returning as Plant and Extrusion Manager.

Sports and Social Club

A thriving Sports and Social Club provided many facilities for enjoyment out of working hours. Football, cricket and tennis teams competed in local leagues and competitions. Events such as athletics, football and cricket matches were enjoyed against other Metal Box Company branches.

Social events, many of which have already been highlighted, included tournaments against local factory teams consisting of table tennis, darts, card games and dominoes. A games room housed a full-size snooker table, which was donated by Mr Mahon, the manager of the local branch of the Midland Bank, in return for favourable custom.

Dances were held at the Palais-de-Dance, on Leeming Street and the Masonic Hall, on Nottingham Road. One of the main sources of revenue for the Sports and Social Committee was the Old Time Dancing Club, very ably run for many years by Eva Shaw and Evelyn Caddy. Dances were held weekly and were particularly popular with company pensioners and their friends. Sadly, these were discontinued during the nineteen-nineties.

CHAPTER TWO

The Evolution of Tin-box Making at Rock Valley and the Development of the Commercial and Business Aspects of the Two Companies.

A well-known parable tells how from the minute mustard seed grew a tree of such fine proportions that the birds of the air were able to shelter amongst its branches. It illustrates that from small beginnings may come great things and the same can be said regarding the evolution of Barringer Wallis and Manners. However, there is an even closer analogy, for the germ of the undertaking may well be said to have begun with mustard seed. Indeed, the business had its inception in the making of tins for the packing of mustard, ground at the 'Mills in Rock Valley.'

Years ago the River Maun provided the motive power for numerous water mills, which straddled its course. Among these was a mill at the lower end of Rock Valley, around which once clustered a range of buildings constructed from local stone quarried from the site where they were subsequently erected. Many and varied were the industries in this little ravine and it is interesting to note that here, around 1815, a workman by the name of James Murray invented the circular saw, which was to revolutionise the timber and wood-working trades.

It is, however, the ancient mustard mill with which we are primarily concerned. Here, David Cooper Barringer began business as a spice and condiment grinder. He obtained the transfer of the lease in 1839, but it is believed that mustard milling had been carried out here as early as 1820. On David Barringer's death, his brother Robert purchased the concern, taking into partnership Edwin Brown of Wakefield and operating under the name of Barringer and Brown.

Mustard was marketed in wooden kegs holding roughly

nine pounds, supplemented by a tin containing four pounds. These tins were made by hand, initially by one man and later by two tinsmiths. It is recorded that in a normal working day of ten hours duration their joint output was forty-eight tins.

The first decoration applied to the tins was 'Black and Gold' and, in 1865 the firm received a gold medal for their exhibit of mustard and mustard tins at the Wakefield Exhibition. The business ticked over until 1873 when fire destroyed many of the buildings in the little colony deep in Rock Valley. The event has been dramatically described by eye-witnesses, but a touch of humour was provided by one of the principal people affected. When called from his bed he was so flustered by the dreadful news that he pulled his trousers on back to front repeatedly! The direct effect of the fire was to provide an opportunity for extension, which was readily seized upon by the proprietors of the mustard mill and the tin shop, whose premises had remained unscathed.

Robert Barringer's son, Walter came from school to enter the firm and, about this time the idea was conceived of opening up a market for tin boxes with decorated surfaces. The premises were extended and, with the increased possibilities thus provided, the addition of colour, by sticking transfer prints onto the tins was experimented with.

Inspired by William Reddan, (initially manager and then outside representative) the first of these decorated seven-pound mustard tins proved a great success. There is no record as to the design that adorned this tin, but several of its successors have survived and they include flowers, children and portraits of the then Prince and Princess of Wales. The latter were reproduced from the coloured photographs that were in vogue at that time.

In 1879 Isaac Henry Wallis joined the firm, which was renamed Barringer and Company. Around 1884 another venture in decoration was launched when a box, having views of the Dukeries (Robin Hood Country) was produced and marketed as 'Sherwood.' This met with a splendid reception and, in 1887 Queen Victoria's Jubilee inspired yet another pictorial box, which again was well received. The foundations for the tin-box side of the firm were definitely laid.

Demand continued to grow and when Robert Barringer retired, in 1889, his place was taken by his son-in-law, Charles Manners, whereupon it was decided to launch a separate undertaking to deal with the tin-box making business. The application of coloured transfers, as in the decorating of pottery, had superceded the sticking on of prints and the next progression, in 1892, was the installation of a lithographic printing plant to produce transfers on the premises.

At that time there were fifty employees and it is interesting to recall that one of the first ventures on the new plant was the black and gold design 'Players Navy Cut.' A century later the firm was still producing tins for the tobacco trade.

The early months of 1893 saw the first machine installed for printing directly onto tinplate sheets. A tin for Gallaghers Rich Dark Honeydew tobacco, decorated with a design by B.Faustin, opened this venture. Success followed success and, in 1895 the company was incorporated under its existing title of Barringer Wallis and Manners.

At that date the number of employees had risen to 143 and tin printing and mustard milling were definitely divorced. The old bleach works in Rock Valley was taken over for tin printing, the mill being devoted entirely to its original business. Some years later the mustard business was sold to the well known firm, Colmans of Norwich. The mill was purchased by Barringer Wallis and Manners and, in common with its neighbours, became an integral part of the tin-box factory.

The demand for more elbow room, combined with the need for a bigger labour market, led to the purchase of a subsidiary factory in Oddicroft Lane, Sutton-in-Ashfield, which has had subsequent extensions added. Growing pains continued to trouble the firm and the various stages of building development can be traced in the long line of premises in Rock Valley ranging from the old stone-built water mill and the single storey workshops, with their expansive roofs of glass and steel, to the four storey Tower Block. The sequence of this building development is as follows:

1909	The 'New Block' as it was then known, which included the canteen.
1918	Acquisition of the Mustard Mill.
1919	The Clock Tower section and Tower Block.
1927	Extension to the Clock Tower section.
1933	North and double storey block
1939/40	New single storey block
1940	Fire Station.

The laying of the foundation stone of the Tower Block was an auspicious event, which attracted considerable local attention. Its completion, together with its clock and weather vane gave Mansfield a new landmark. However, the high watermark was reached in June 1914 when the firm was honoured by the visit of King George V and Queen Mary, accompanied by the Duke and Duchess of Portland and other influential members of the royal circle.

Barringer Wallis and Manners were justly proud of the fact that they were the only tin-box manufacturers to be granted a succession of Royal Warrants. These were bestowed by Queen Victoria, Edward VII, George V, Queen Mary and King Albert I of Belgium.

Another honour was the following series of royal boxes that were commissioned:

Queen Victoria's chocolate tin, which was sent to the troops during the South African War.

Princess Mary's Gift Box, presented to members of the expeditionary force at Christmas 1914.

Souvenir tins made for Edward VII and Queen Alexandra.

Coronation tins made over the period from Edward VII to George VI.

The tin celebrating the wedding of the Duke and Duchess of York (George VI and Queen Elizabeth).

One branch of the firm's activities, the manufacture of children's toys, was launched as a direct outcome of the First World War. When supplies from abroad dried up it was decided to try and meet the demand by home production. In consequence, clockwork motor cars, engines, aeroplanes, weapons and numerous other contrivances, guaranteed to delight children, were manufactured at these works.

The hallmark of the firm has been its splendid design and workmanship. Not only have highly qualified designers been employed in the Artists' studios, but engineering craftsmen, who developed the press tools, were of the finest calibre. Attention to detail was borne out by the meticulous presentation of hand-made models, decorated by the Artists' Department. They were displayed for customer approval, like jewellery, on a background of blue velvet. When a sample or model was sent to a customer it was packed in a made-to-measure, stout cardboard box, complete with a Barringer Wallis and Manners gold medallion. These cardboard boxes were made by Edna Allcock, sister to Molly who worked in Commercial.

One of the earliest examples of collaboration between manufacturer and artist is demonstrated in the old 'Alice in Wonderland' box, produced after consultation with Lewis Carroll, the author of the world-renowned story. (See Appendix 2 for correspondence from the author to the company concerning this and other products manufactured for him). Shapes too have played an important part in product development and, with self-contained model-making and design workshops, continual experimentation has been possible in an effort to produce a continuous flow of new and attractive forms.

Perhaps the most outstanding achievement in this direction has been the perfection of a process for giving a contour to the walls of round or faceted tins, generally known as 'bulging' and referred to in Chapter One. Regular experimentation in the field of printing and surface finishes has also been carried out, culminating in the attractive 'ripple' designs, which were launched at the outbreak of the Second World War. Reproduction processes too were kept under review and developments in natural colour photography have been utilised as they became practical. In both World Wars the resources of the Mansfield and Sutton-in-Ashfield works were placed at the Government's disposal for the manufacture of supplies essential to the war effort.

A measure of the scale of increased production in the early years can be obtained by comparing the two tinsmiths turning out 48 hand-made tins per day with the annual output of over 100,000,000 containers and other articles, immediately prior to the Second World War.

Decorated tin boxes, although manufactured in vast quantities and exported around the world, are by no means the only style of containers the firm has produced. In addition, advertising tablets, shelf strips, ashtrays, string boxes, display stands, calendars and hardware items figure amongst other products. Many of these items have been exported, particularly to Canada, USA, Australia and South Africa.

There was keen competition in the General Line tin-box field from the beginning of the twentieth century, with relatively little mechanisation or rationalisation and hand presses playing a significant role in operations. Barringer Wallis and Manners had built up a good reputation in the confectionery, biscuit, pharmaceutical, toiletries and advertising sphere, striving for the highest quality and probably unequalled in the complexity of articles produced.

Competition became particularly acute after the First World War with relative slumps and it was this that led to considerable rationalisation, although individual firms preserved their originality. During the 1930's the Metal Box Company was growing and developing under the direction of Sir Robert Barlow. It is concluded that competition, particularly with Hudson Scott of Carlisle, who were amongst the founder members of the Company, began to hurt Barringer Wallis and Manners to the degree that they joined the fold in 1939.

The foundation of the Extrusion business was laid at Rock Valley during the 1930's when it was decided to enter the collapsible tube field. Presses and printing equipment were installed and production began on Gibbs Dentifrice tubes, which were made from pure tin at that time. Development was halted due to the outbreak of war, but some of the same equipment was used when aluminium extrusion began in 1945.

Under the major reorganisation following the Second World War a considerable rearrangement of operations ensued. Printing activity was transferred from the Tower

Block to Sutton-in-Ashfield. Up to that time all tinplate sheets were printed on flat-bed machines and hung to allow them to air dry. The Sutton plant was adapted to house rotary printing machines and travelling drying ovens, representing a considerable step forward. Also, the manufacture of an extensive range of metal toys for Chad Valley was concentrated at Sutton, thus enabling the Mansfield site to rearrange its production facilities and to concentrate on its high quality containers, for which the old cramped buildings were not suited. The move freed around 12,000 square feet of floor space in Tower Block, which was filled with improved production lines for talcum and seamless tobacco tins. One floor was devoted to metal advertising display tablets and stands, in addition to dispenser units and novelties.

In 1947 advantage was taken of spare land at the Sutton site to build a somewhat utility Open Top factory, utilising equipment transferred from Aintree, with the aim of supplying cans to Batchelor's Peas of Sheffield, which, like Sutton, was rail connected. Bulk tinplate came from Neath in South Wales direct to the Sutton site. This formed the main supply for both Mansfield and Sutton.

In 1953 a further fourteen acres, additional to the ten already owned, were purchased, which allowed the later building of a new printing factory, incorporating the latest printing technology. This purchase also provided space for an excellent sports-ground that was used for a variety of activities, including horticultural shows.

During the period between 1947 and 1953 tinplate became rationed due to acute shortages. The demand for decorated boxes remained high and aluminium was utilised. Confectionery and biscuit business boomed and the demand for Coronation souvenir tins was so great in 1953 that a factory at Leicester was purchased by the Metal Box Company, in order to supplement production. Some tray business and associated equipment was transferred to Liverpool and the smaller diameter range of extruded tube business went to the Hull factory.

In the immediate post-war period the Metal Box Company manufactured its first aerosol containers in Rock

Valley. They had a shallow aluminium extruded body, which was closed after filling by seaming on a concave end in which a valve had already been soldered. Early in the 1950's the current design was adopted, which incorporated closure by crimping a cup holding a valve in the standard aperture. Sadly, the Extrusion Department made little progress with Monobloc aerosols and many of its staple types - containers for pharmaceuticals and 35 m/m films - moved to plastic. It was therefore ripe for a management buyout and life as Ashfield Extrusion, that came about in the 1960's.

The post-war boom in decorated boxes passed and competition from alternative packaging was growing. By the mid-1950's Mansfield and Sutton sites felt its cold breeze, which had been absent for almost twenty years. The major casualty, representing the growth of pre-packed foods and the increasing cost of hand packing and dispensing, was the returnable standard biscuit tin. This container, which kept two production lines in constant use at Rock Valley from shortly after the Second World War, was eventually phased out in the mid 1960's. An alternative container of the same dimensions, but of easier construction, was developed alongside the original and still sells in a specially decorated presentation form. However, the large tinplate biscuit container has been superceded, although its life was extended briefly by its use for holding packets of potato crisps. These are now packaged in cardboard containers.

Between 1954 and 1961 the demand for fancy boxes declined drastically with many customers heavily over-stocked. A downturn in business conducted with Imported Delicacies of New York and Chad Valley also affected profitability. A wide range of products was discontinued and Mansfield was relieved to receive some production from the Portslade factory, which had converted to injection-moulding of plastics.

The worrying trend led to a period of retrenchment and the end of the seller's market brought a continual and enthusiastic search for economies and new business. Labour savings included a reduction in the number of personal secretaries and other staff. On the positive side there was some improvement in advertising business, notably an order for 300,000 McVitie's tablets, displaying the slogan, 'Say McVitie.' The Champion Spark Plug 'Plugometer,' a tinplate holder for sellotape, formed another stop-gap remedy. Very substantial stock-piling, by the Ministry of Food, of margarine and biscuit tins led to enormous demand for 9¼ square containers that carried the Mansfield factory through several winters, whilst the traditional summer and autumn peak trade for confectionery and biscuit tins continued its steady decline. Industrial component outlets were actively sought without a full appreciation of the uncertainty of repeat orders and the stringent requirements regarding decoration and tolerances.

In 1961, at a particularly inauspicious moment, the AEU presented a wage demand to the Company for a sixpence an hour all-round increase for its members. This action had no precedent and, almost by mistake, a realistic offer was rejected and all the engineers went on strike. Thanks to dedicated service by supervision and tool-setters, production continued for three weeks with relatively little disruption amidst uncertainty as to the stoppage being official or unofficial. The matter was finally resolved following a meeting between Head Office representatives and the Union Executive Committee when agreement was reached to end the strike. The engineers returned to work having suffered financially and with considerable ill-feeling regarding the settlement.

A short-lived boom in the national economy suggested that the company's General Line production capacity was inadequate and created a climate for the provision of a new building. The old Sutton-in-Ashfield Printing Department was an obvious candidate for re-housing, in view of the considerable fire hazard and the impossibility of installing the longer ovens required to accommodate the larger tinplate sheet sizes which were becoming available from the improved steel plants in South Wales. In the light of this a new Printing Factory was constructed at Sutton, which provided 40,000 square feet of manufacturing space and allowed the installation of equipment additional to the printing lines. The aluminium extrusion production was transferred to this area from Mansfield, which created enough space there to bring the remnants of tin-box making from Sutton. The old buildings at Sutton that had housed the General Line manufacture were converted to warehousing, for which they had originally been designed.

In 1960 a decision was made to make the Extrusion Department a separate entity under a departmental manager and a supporting staff, so that its destiny could be more readily achieved. This move was clearly justified by 1964, but only after difficulties, caused by the upheaval of transferring the business to Sutton, had been overcome.

The economic climate changed unfortunately as building commenced, necessitating the delay of non-immediate requirements. The range of offices at the front of the building was designed to incorporate a second floor, but only a section of this upper floor was constructed, in order to house the Reproduction Department. Non-co-operation by the Society of Lithographic Artists at that time led to the establishment of an Artists' studio at the Leicester factory instead of at Sutton, as had been originally planned.

The building project fell behind schedule and, instead of the transfer of equipment happening during a quiet period, it took place at a time of peak production for both printing and extrusion. Printing was aggravated by having to operate in both shops for a considerable period without additional services or supervision and with exceptional teething troubles on the oven unloaders. The consequences in terms of spoilage, poor efficiency, broken promises and changes to planned production programmes were amply reflected in the company's results. In 1963 further retrenchment was attempted and a number of marginal performers on the staff were asked to leave. The annual salary review was postponed for three months until it could take place against a more encouraging background. A series of quarterly meetings was instituted for monthly-salaried and supervisory staff in order to keep them informed during the difficult period. Subsequently, as part of a more liberal policy regarding the dissemination of information, a Weekly News Sheet was developed.

Further rationalisation took place in 1963 when the tray business, which had been transferred to the Liverpool factory, was returned to Mansfield. At the same time some unprofitable talcum business, due to limited bodymaker capacity, was shed to Carlisle. This was followed in 1964 by the decision to close the Providence Works at Worcester and transfer the bulk of the Hardware business to Mansfield, whose traditional confectionery and biscuit tin trade was declining. Major factors in the decline were difficulties involved in packing gift packs on high-speed lines and a tighter link between Huntley Boorne and Stevens and five of the major biscuit manufacturers.

At this time Open Top required additional space at Sutton for expansion and storage and it was arranged to extend the old General Line factory (Toy Factory) to provide a convenient warehouse and distribution centre. To meet the needs of the Hardware business at Mansfield, two tennis courts, which had been provided in 1924, were sacrificed for the siting of an additional storage building.

A determined effort was made to expand the Hardware business by the introduction of consumer advertising - the development of supplementary business by the production of known lines for stores through premium gift promoters. The manufacture of drink mats, table mats and canisters at Mansfield became extremely significant economically, as did the associated increase in printing activity. A Hardware Supplies Manager was appointed to co-ordinate production, storage and distribution of this important facet of the business.

By chance a visitor from Thomassen and Drijver remarked how much he preferred to make 100,000 Luncheon Boxes every four years, as a premium gift, to selling 20,000 a year through normal retail outlets. This led to the exploration of doing likewise in the UK. Unilever were approached initially but their company structure presented difficulties. Fortunately, their rivals, Proctor and Gamble, were much more approachable and an inquiry for 5,000,000 table mats was obtained, to be delivered over thirteen weeks and starting in eight. The scale and precision of the operation was way beyond anything Mansfield had experienced and some said that taking on such business would ruin the Metal Box Company's reputation and the branch's mat prospects. The alternative to such an opportunity was not to be contemplated and the challenge was accepted and successfully overcome. At the last count 35,000,000 table mats had been made for the premium gift market, together with a further ten products for Proctor and Gamble. Benefits spilled over to other Metal Box branches and into a whole range of premium packages for customers in Europe and the USA. An additional outcome was the creation of better ways of tooling and manufacturing traditional fancy boxes

Gradually, the new printing factory's efficiency improved and spare capacity became available. The decline in Batchelor's Peas can requirements led the Open Top factory to convert some equipment for the manufacture of tinplate aerosol bodies and this business expanded significantly, including a substantial proportion of decorated bodies. It was agreed that the printing of these should be undertaken by the new printing factory. Thus, by 1964 a quarter of the production from this factory went to Open Top, which, as part of a separate Group within the Metal Box Company, assumed a major position amongst the branch's customers. In 1965 a Printing Manager was appointed, following a two-year gap after the retirement of Walter Ormston, to ensure a good service by the factory to Open Top and Mansfield. He would also oversee the significant resource of plate making and reproduction that was supplied to the Poole factory.

The absorption of Hardware production from Providence Works led to considerable reorganisation at Mansfield in 1964, which allowed the growth of the significant seamless cigar tin business. This justified the installation of semi-automatic production lines in the first floor of the Tower Block. A complication was the decision of all customers to simultaneously change to a tin with a curled lid and body at a period of ever-increasing demand.

An increase in the share of business obtained from Johnson and Johnson, for baby powder and 'Band-Aid' tins, led to two further high-speed lines being installed in the top floor of the Tower Block alongside the existing lines producing talcum powder tins.

The production supplied by the above high-speed production lines was relatively unaffected by seasonal demand and had the advantage of long runs due to a small number of customers being responsible for a large proportion of the output. Accordingly, this business provided a welcome boost to the workload of the factory.

Very little satisfactory work endured at this time on industrial components, with the exception of the CAV oil filter can and the butane gas cartridge. Increasing price competition regarding trays in Middle East markets led to the Press Shop being ripe for re-development and a significant new source of business was sought. This was found in the form of film and printing ink canisters, produced to high specifications and in large quantities.

During the period from 1967 to 1974 three catastrophic events affected the Metal Box Company, both at local level and nationally. The first was the horrendous fire at the Sutton-in-Ashfield Printing factory, which caused the virtual destruction of the Printing and Reproduction Departments. As the Mansfield factory received its complete supply of printed tinplate from Sutton, a major operation was instigated to keep it afloat with alternative supplies from other Metal Box factories.

A massive rebuilding plan was approved and put into operation with staff recruited mainly from Mansfield to deal with the installation of new plant and machinery. Other Metal Box factories helped with the reproduction process and, as with the much earlier fire that destroyed buildings in Rock Valley, the Printing factory rose like a phoenix from the ashes.

The opportunity to modernise was grasped and buildings, designed to accept the latest printing machinery and tinplate handling systems, were constructed, also incorporating a new Reproduction Department. New warehouses were built, including the replacement of the old Toy Factory that had formerly housed the General Line production and had been affected by the fire. The latest mechanical handling aids were utilised in these new premises.

The Sutton site was restored to full production in record time and, despite numerous difficulties, all the staff involved did a first-class job. However, at the end of 1968 a second fire, which was confined to the extract ducting in the Printing Department, halted production of printed tinplate once again. Mansfield engineers were called upon to re-design the extraction system and some members of the Mansfield staff were transferred to Sutton at that time on a permanent basis.

In 1974 came the three-day working week, when the whole country was affected by the coal miners' strike. Stocks of tinplate were severely depleted and the Production Control departments were at full stretch trying to locate surplus or non-urgent stocks in order to complete contracts. Eventually, production returned to normal, but change came in the form of mass-produced aerosol containers. The new invention of soudronically welded tinplate proved a revolution and was incorporated into aerosol manufacture. It also opened up new techniques in the production of tinplate and heavier gauge metal containers. The Sutton factory was to become one of the leading suppliers of first-class, soudronically welded containers, manufactured on fully automated production lines on an around the clock basis. Some specialised containers, incorporating the same process, were made at Mansfield for a period. These included tennis ball holders and hair lacquer receptacles. Some notable management staff at Sutton at that time was as follows: Factory Managers, J.Eadie and A.Roberts. Personnel, J.Bowkett. Supervisors, H.Richards, J. Flaherty, T.Gibson, N.Pierce, T.Stubbs and W.Bailey. Foremen, L.Frith, P.Hoare, E.Roberts, K.Dawn, A.Kirk, E.Sleigh, M.Ward, R.Else and S.Johnson. Tool-setters, L.Else, C.Carling and R.Hurst. Surgery, Sister Gregory.

When the old Toy factory at Sutton became used for Worcester Ware storage, packing and despatch, the staff involved was as follows: Manager, J.Langford, assisted by Ralph Stone. Chris Kinghorn was in charge of Buying and the Purchasing Assistant was Joan Bull (Abbott). Forewoman, Elsie Richardson and one of the female packers was E.Barker.

CHAPTER THREE

Products and Customers

In a special catalogue, issued in 1915/1916 eight premier decorated containers were listed, as follows:

'Moscow' Handkerchief Box.

'Petrograd' Glove Box.

'Fireside' Vase.

'National' Caddy, so called because portraits of English, Irish, Welsh and Scottish beauties were featured on it. This was produced in three sizes.

'Warfare' Box, a caddy type container in two sizes, decorated in two colours and depicting modern warfare.

'Fables' Box, a caddy type, offered in two sizes, its design representing 'Aesop's Fables.'

'Telephone Call' Box, probably a moneybox, three and a quarter inches square.

'British Empire' Box, sold in four sizes.

The most expensive item of the above was eightpence, (a little more than 3P!)

The period from 1930 to the 1980's saw a vast change in fancy-box design and manufacture. Biscuit and tea companies and the confectionery trade were demanding better quality containers in respect of design, shape and decoration. Stock boxes and design ranges were introduced to cut costs on large orders for seasonal requirements. Many of these designs were the copyright of Barringer Wallis and Manners.

Companies such as the Co-operative Wholesale Society (CWS), Jacobs, Crawfords, Huntley and Palmers, Peek Freans, Carrs, McVitie and Price, McFarlane-Lang and Fox's Biscuits were in the market for a range of fancy containers with shapes that would attract the public and encourage them to purchase the contents. Some customers ordered a different shaped container on a yearly basis whereas others merely changed the artwork. Many of these products had an after use as storage for sugar, flour or rice and some were even supplied with a small tinplate scoop.

Meredith and Drew, along with the CWS (Crumpsall), Elkes Biscuits and Kemps Biscuits were supplied with the large square biscuit tins, holding approximately seven pounds. These were often referred to as 'bread and butter products,' some being fitted with a glass lid, to allow inspection of the contents.

Another long-running staple product of this style was the 91/4 inch margarine tin sold to Vandenburgs and the Ministry of Food for strategic stockpile.

A varied range of containers was manufactured for the confectionery companies, the largest being a bow-sided tin with a screw-top lid for holding Nuttall's Mintoes. Large chocolate boxes were made for companies such as Cadburys, Mackintosh's, Rowntrees, Terrys and Cravens of York, Trebor, Sharps, Needlers, Caleys and the distinctive silver and blue tins for Harrogate toffee. This business also embraced advertising plaques of varying sizes and dispensers, for which a department was created, the output being so large.

These advertising aids displayed trade names such as Reckitt and Coleman, Crosse and Blackwell, Cerebos, Michelin and Champion, which utilised the skill in toolmaking for embossed products that had been developed for earlier container designs.

Products were produced over the years that served to protect a multitude of universally marketed commodities. In addition to the above mentioned fancy boxes, food containers and advertising matter, tins were manufactured to hold items as diverse as the following:

Tobacco, cigarettes, cigars, snuff, pills, powder, health salts, tooth powder, ointment, pastilles and lozenges, talcum powder, hair oil, soap, pen nibs, pins, paper clips, gramophone needles, typewriter ribbons, screws, nails, springs, repair outfits, plugs and polish. Money-boxes, first aid tins, collection boxes and cases added to the extensive range.

A popular type of the tins used to contain powder was the Talcum tin, which provided a good source of business. The main customers were Coty, Yardleys, Boots, Revlon,

Cussons, and Johnson and Johnson. This style of tin was manufactured to a high standard of decoration and tightness of the seams.

The most remarkable of the products for industrial use were, perhaps, nuclear fuel rod containers, whose contamination by gold had to be avoided. This resulted in married women involved in their production having to remove their wedding rings!

A significant contribution to the Hardware business was made in 1964 by David Hicks, who was acutely critical of the company's designs on such products. They were based on colour transparencies of 'Old Masters' and sentimental subjects. David inquired if he could feature some of the designs in a television programme he was compiling concerning reprehensible British design. The company agreed, subject to his producing better designs, which were saleable. This led to the first 'Textile' design on hardware, which took advantage of a batch of reproduction work for a range of 'Colourways.' The initial design for 'Goods and Chattels' proved very expensive to produce due to a long, black panel, which showed every blemish. By contrast the remainder was not so difficult and the concept was adopted. The decorated tinware achieved significant popularity, not least in 'Swinging' London's Carnaby Street.

During a depressed sales period, in the spring of 1964 it was decided to print a tray featuring The Beatles, just as they had achieved national fame, or notoriety, depending on your viewpoint. Unimaginatively, it displayed merely their individual portraits, which was due to the perceived need for maximum speed from conception to sale. This was attributable to paranoia regarding the possibility of their death, or dishonour rendering the complete, uninsured stock a write-off. 180,000 were manufactured and sold, but no more editions were considered. However, the tray has become a collector's item and presently trades at £100/£150!

Reference has already been made to Biscuit Tins and their original standard designs being phased out in the 1960's. Fortunately, through the ceaseless search for innovation, in a climate of constant change, the standard 'seated-in bottom, wired top' version had begun a series of metamorphoses. For speed of manufacture and increased protection from air and water, Alan Cowan had developed a double-seamed version. This was rejected by the major biscuit manufacturers, but it was taken on board by Meredith and Drew, so that it became unfairly known as their tin, rather than the generic successor to the original model. It only achieved general acceptance in the half, or lesser depth, which led to the creation of the 'TV', or 'Quartic' shape by Cyril Bull and the design team. Numerous models were made, but eventually this product became a winner with its improved 'sealed-in bottom,' die-curled body and lid that allowed a perfect fit between them. It lent itself to mass production and was destined to survive for many decades.

The 'Cleanline' range of containers was initiated by the idea of assembling two identical stampings with inward curls to form a coffret or chocolate box with maximum display area and minimum reproduction and printing costs. The construction was completed by a vacuum-formed insert, or a plastic or composite ring. The lid had an after use as a wall decoration and the container was ideal for taping to give a long shelf life to the contents. Unfortunately, the concept only materialised in the form of a built up canister that never moved beyond the mark one model. However, what did emerge, and is still called 'Cleanline,' was a round built up canister with a single shell, stepped and inwardly curled lid, which was bulged to match the outside diameter of the body, to allow taping. As it was relatively cheap to manufacture, other models were envisaged incorporating such features as a tear-out diaphragm. The idea provided impetus to the sale of quality and premium containers sold empty or for refills and dispelled the notion that customers and consumers were interested only in cheapness.

Thomas Nutbrown desired a cheaper tray to provide the two platforms of a folding trolley and Mansfield tried to compensate for the lightening of the material by curling its edges. The result had so much whip it was rejected by the customer, who refused to pay for the tooling. Left with expendable tools, the engineers experimented with putting two thin sheets of tinplate through a set of tools designed for one thick sheet and seeing how readily they were subsequently curled together, separated by a deadening distance piece. The idea was successful and provided a useful outlet for some sub-standard decorated tinplate. It could have been sold in this form had the product been suitably priced. However, I recall a similar version being produced, in the form of a double-shell tray with a fibre insert, which rendered it heat proof, in addition to a quality feel. I believe C.I.Mellor conceived the idea of fitting three brass-plated legs, approximately twelve inches long, to a tray of this type that was twelve inches in diameter. An ingenious idea, it made a perfect occasional drinks table and I still have one in use. From memory I am reasonably certain a substantial order was obtained for a tray of this type, with and without legs.

Over the years there were frequent innovative failures, mainly due to lack of resources or commitment. Unfortunately, there is little record of them, which may have been of benefit if the climate improved, marketability and profit-wise. A puff-lined coaster for glasses and wine bottles is an example of such failure. However, stainless steel was experimented with in order to use up some obsolete printing plates and this proved successful. It also demonstrated how a curl compensated for thinner material plates and trays.

In a slightly different category of failures was the 'strip-seal' end, for which the original assembly machine was developed at Mansfield in 1957, However. It was transferred to the Neath factory when there appeared no way in which Mansfield could benefit from the development, beyond its application for lubricating-oil can tops.

The diversity of toys produced at Mansfield and Sutton-in-Ashfield deserves mention, particularly in terms of inventiveness and creativity. Consider the overhead railway sets, the control car, which incorporated a governed clockwork motor that operated for almost two minutes. Constructed from die-cast aluminium, the car was controlled by a hand-held rubber bulb, which, when squeezed, turned it to the left or right. Figure of eight train sets also featured, as did coaches and station buildings. There were humming tops that changed tune, aeroplanes and model boats, which, I believe, had a small steam boiler, heated by a small candle in a tray. Amongst many other varieties were building bricks, world globes with stand, buses and trams. It is true to say that at least one hundred female operatives were engaged in toy making at Mansfield and Sutton-in-Ashfield, making the factories a major supplier before and after the Second World War.

CHAPTER FOUR

Works Committee and Trade Union Involvement

The Metal Box Company introduced an Employees' Works Committee Charter, in 1946 I believe. The structure of the Works Committee for the Mansfield and Sutton-in-Ashfield sites has been outlined in Chapter One. All committee members were free from discrimination and its constitution was equal in gender. It was an excellent body, for it kept the workforce informed of the workload and future prospects of the two factories.

Each meeting was chaired by the General Manager, or, in his absence, the Factory Manager. On the agenda were reports from the departmental sub-committees. These were as follows:

Engineering - given by the Chief Engineer, Health and Safety - given by Bert Britcliffe or Tom Foden, Canteen - given by the Canteen Manager, Sports and Social - given by the Personnel Officer.

The factory Benevolent and Charities Committee report was given by its chairman, Ted Backus or myself and its contribution was important. This committee dealt with public money and approval was required by the full Works Committee when external charities applied for assistance. Also, grants for hardship were put forward for action and approval.

Reports from the Production Control Department were given by R.Mitchell or Brian Hall, which provided a review of the future workload, backed up by reports from all the Departmental Production Supervisors. In addition, factory social events were discussed and a talk was given by the management, with no bars to questions from committee members present.

I am thankful for the foresight of the Metal Box Company Chairman, Sir Robert Barlow and his brother, Ernest, for sanctioning the setting up of such committees when they charted the future direction of the Company.

It is appropriate to mention the involvement of the trade unions within the Mansfield and Sutton-in-Ashfield sites, beginning in the early 1900's. At that time engineers were members of the Amalgamated Society of Engineers, an elite organisation that recruited highly skilled craftsmen and bound apprentices. The latter served a seven-year apprenticeship and had to abide by a strict set of rules. The engineers were proud of their skill and protected their rights with vigour. At the time of the First World War there was a need to recruit semi-skilled engineers and a new section of the Union was established with limited benefits. In the 1930's the Union was re-named the Amalgamated Engineering Union (AEU) and all the engineers employed by Barringer Wallis and Manners were encouraged to join this body. It was a very democratic organisation, with regular fortnightly branch meetings.

A register of skills was established at branch level and when vacancies occurred in the area members were notified together with details of rates of pay and conditions offered. Letters of recommendation to an employer were also supplied and it was not surprising that toolmakers, skilled in certain types of precision engineering, moved within the industry in order to gain advancement. Thus, a pool of very skilled workers was created, which was quite elitist and tended to favour a closed shop.

Nationally, the AEU moved quickly to organise the engineering workforce. New branches were formed and district office staff was engaged. A high-quality education programme was put into operation for all elected full-time officers and shop stewards. This included university and college residential summer courses, with lectures regarding company accounts and balance sheets, employment law and health and safety. Courses were also run by the Workers' Education Association, the National Council of Labour Colleges and the Trades Union Council.

The AEU Executive Council appointed full-time officers

responsible for each of the engineering industries. In the case of a multi-national company, there could be an Executive Council member responsible for that particular company in National Agreement negotiations, as was the case with the Metal Box Company.

From the mid 1950's regular meetings of shop stewards and convenors representing all twenty-seven factories within the Metal Box Company were held in London, attended by a full-time Executive Council member. The agenda covered wages and conditions, shift and overtime-premium payments, pensions, health and safety and time off work for trade union and civic duties.

A Shop Stewards' Combined Committee was appointed to monitor individual factory trends concerning the above matters. This was a self-financing and consultative body, which became a recognised organisation by resolution to the AEU National Committee in 1969. It was established quickly that, in order to make progress on rates of pay and conditions and, most importantly, maximise pensions, there was a need to standardise the wide variety of rates of pay pertaining in the various factories. A programme was instigated to reduce the number of rates of pay to three - a starting rate, intermediate rate (flexible to take account of training and transfers) and a top rate, which was normally paid within five years.

The progression towards this structure could only be done in stages, as it was necessary to change working practices and shift patterns to achieve higher productivity. There were many conflicts and hurdles to be overcome, sometimes resulting in industrial action, but the AEU officials realised the importance of a reasonable company pension, to enhance the inadequate state pension. The only way to achieve this was to make the pension scheme contributions affordable for all members by a progression in hourly rates of pay.

The Metal Box Company had a first-class employee pension scheme, together with an excellent sickness benefit scheme for long-term employees and the rate of pay had a bearing on both of these. These fringe benefits were greatly appreciated by the factory workforce, particularly female members who attended hospital for further tests following cancer-screening sessions at the Medical Centre.

Employee and pensioner representatives were eventually elected, democratically, to the Board of Pension Trustees and progress reports from the central committee to pensioners, containing a statement of accounts, are commonplace.

Amongst other trade unions having agreements with the Metal Box Company were those of the Transport and General Workers and the General and Municipal Workers. These unions negotiated broadly for factory operatives generally employed in semi-skilled occupations, but some employees were classed as skilled and paid the appropriate rate. A major step forward was achieved in 1975 when female production workers were allowed to join the company pension scheme.

Print workers, artists, Reproduction Department, clerical and Drawing Office staff were also members of their appropriate trade unions. Like the AEU there were strict rules of entry to these disciplined organisations and its members were proud of their professional skills, which warranted high rates of pay. All unions had national wage and conditions agreements, with those of the Transport and General Workers and the Municipal Workers probably being the most comprehensive.

Relations between the various unions was good and they often co-operated to ensure efficient production levels were maintained. The relationship between them and the two companies (Barringer Wallis and Manners and the Metal Box Company) was generally favourable, due, no doubt to compromise on both sides.

As a result of the need to reduce capacity the Metal Box Company negotiated a redundancy agreement, which allowed long-serving employees to benefit by taking early retirement, a major step forward in industrial relations. Similarly the unions needed to overhaul their structure due to shrinking markets and overlapping interests. Eventually various unions amalgamated and the AEU combined with Electrical and Plumbers Trade Union to become the Amalgamated Engineering and Electrical Union (AEEU).

CHAPTER FIVE

Additional Notes on Factors Affecting the Commercial Operations of the Metal Box Company

The following notes are a continuation of a history of the Metal Box Company written in 1965 when C.I.Mellor ceased to be General Manager of the Mansfield and Sutton-in-Ashfield factories. The history was compiled when Metal Box may have been in its prime, with some sixty plants in the United Kingdom, of which twelve were in the Open Top Group. The latter were managed to a large degree by Factory Managers, under central control from Acton, London. Another twelve were 'General Line,' in the main the original 'tin-box makers' of the 1920's, run by General Managers with their own Commercial and Production Control functions, loosely co-ordinated by the London Headquarters of the Company.

Outside the range of these notes were the Paper and Plastic Groups, Machinery Building Group and some centralised accounting, personnel and administration elements and the Overseas Division. At this time the Metal Box Company had 55,000 employees, but sadly, few entrepreneurs with foresight and awareness of impending dramatic changes due to new technology. Exciting innovations were appearing, such as the two-piece can, aluminium challenging tinplate, and plastics and cardboard challenging both of these. Another disturbing situation was the invasion of the UK by American companies, with Continental Can being provoked by Metal Box opening a beverage container factory in California.

A section of the Hardware business, 'Consumer Products' Kitchen Giftware, was given a substantial transfusion by the acquisition from the liquidator of 'Tala' (Taylor Law, of Blackpool) and the imagination of its Metal

Box manager who was allowed to buy it out. He earned a good living from the business and ultimately sold it. 'Tala' is currently based in Leiston, Suffolk, with its last ex-Sutton Metal Box employee retiring in 2003.

Around 1973 a substantial change took place at Sutton-in-Ashfield, occasioned by General Line Group being required to release two top executives. These were the only ones, apart from the Group Manager, to have experience of the 'White Cap' business at Poole, with its substantial mainland business and crucial Continental Can licenses. It was accepted that General Line and Open Top Groups would exchange business (White Caps and aerosols), so that Poole would answer to Peter Hewett, who was moving to Open Top Group as Commercial Manager.

By that time, Mansfield already had a toe hold in the aerosol business. It had taken the tennis ball tin business from the Hull branch when it moved from soldered to welded construction and thus into pressure containers for butane gas and cheap fire extinguishers and, incidentally, establishing the first link with Swiss Soudronic AG.

Within Metal Box, especially Neath branch and also BSC, a series of strikes had encouraged a policy of two sources of supply, however vulnerable, and aerosol lines had been installed at Rochester branch. These were moved to Sutton-in-Ashfield, which also became self sufficient for cones and domes and acquired its own commercial function and opportunity for innovation. First, however, came the need to move to welded bodies despite the USA's move towards two-piece bodies. A year passed before agreement came from 'on high' to purchase high-speed soudronic welding machines. The desirability of a second source of supply in the event of emergency, was met by seeking Johnson's recommendations, which led to the acquisition of San Ilario in Italy by 'Superbox', Metal Box's operation in that country.

There was still significant aluminium aerosol business to chase and it was suggested that the tinplate version's appearance would be enhanced by 'necking in' top and bottom, using beverage can equipment. This development was a great success, for the previous double seams scuffed the decoration of adjacent cans. Also, material savings were achieved in end manufacture and there was an eight-percent increase in the number of containers on a pallet.

Johnson's Wax, a major customer, was not prepared to change unless other suppliers, like Crown Cork, did. They tried using Krupp equipment, but failed until Metal Box supplied them with suitable machines. The promotional cans produced also featured embossed bodies, (probably de-bossed to avoid scuffing in transit). This simple possibility, with its advantage over aluminium extrusions, never took off, or so I believe.

Nor were other possibilities explored. There was hope that Portslade's valve production might have been moved to Mansfield and that the interface between valve plus mounting cap and body might have been made more economical (as the earliest Metal Box aerosol). This may have been related to the export of aerosols for local filling in minor overseas markets where Metal Box Overseas Division could have welcomed more business, especially as a weapon against the mosquito. Then two-piece tapered and stepped bodies could have been economically transported and closed by a seamed-on end, or through an end hole and rubber plug. So much for dreams of the 1980's, recalled in 2004.

This ends, as do my original notes, with the hope that others will update the history for their successors and be mindful of the extent to which product innovation and change in organisation may be needed to see off competition.

(C.I.Mellor 2004)

Afterword

It is hoped that this book is of historical interest and provides an insight into factory life, conditions of employment and the progress of product technology from 1895 to 1983. Many former employees have indicated that it would be gratifying to remember the good times enjoyed by the workforce and especially the characters that made working at Barringer Wallis and Manners and the Metal Box Company a pleasure they will always hold dear. The following responses to this book are hopefully a testament to this view.

What memories your production brings to life, especially of a bygone age, when I, a bachelor youngster, moved from Cromwell's fenland to the Royalist Dukeries. I transferred from a young new factory to one steeped in history with such a seasoned management. I quickly acquired a brilliant wife, and so two extra eyes and ears, and a partner for splendid staff dinner-dances and Sports and Social functions. These occasions were a feature of those times, when Mansfield and Sutton's payroll numbered some 3,000, including such notables as Ondrey Allsopp and Stan Bellamy : no computers or mobile phones!
C.I.Mellor

Out of the hundreds, nay thousands of individuals with whom we came into contact, there are many more than those named in this book who made their contribution to the life and success of the Company. Many names spring to mind - for instance, I recall a lady on the cleaning staff (a 'Mrs. Mop') - Mrs. Strauther was her name. The pleasant part is that one can recall them with regard and affection.
J.E.Walsh

Appendices

1 Extract from the Mansfield Advertiser, Friday March 7th 1873, concerning the fire in Rock Valley.

2 History of 'The Looking Glass' Box - Including letters from C.L.Dodgson (Lewis Caroll) to Miss Mary E.Manners and Mr Charles Manners in 1891 and 1892. (4 Pages)

3 Invitations to the Annual Dinner of Barringer Wallis and Manners employees in 1899 and the Foundation Stone Laying of the Rock Valley Works extension in 1919.

4 Visit of King George V and Queen Mary to Mansfield and the Rock Valley Works in 1914, including the itinerary, plan of the route and letters from the King and Buckingham Palace. (6 Pages)

5 Poster for St. Dunstans Hostel and Concert at Arcadia Hall.

6 Extracts from a Mansfield 'Reporter' article of 1927 concerning the extension to the Tower Block of the Rock Valley Works.

7 Letter from the Joint Managing Director of Barringer Wallis and Manners, dated July 1939, concerning arrangements to associate the firm with the Metal Box Company.

8 Barringer Wallis and Manners - Some notable dates. (2 Pages)

9 Joyce Bryan's Wartime Memories of the Metal Box Company (formerly Barringer Wallis and Manners).

Extract from Mansfield Advertiser, Friday March 7th 1873

FATEFUL FIRE AT MANSFIELD

ROCK VALLEY MILLS COMPLETELY GUTTED

Between three and four o'clock this morning the Wood Yard and Bobbin Shop occupied by Mr.Pye were discovered to be on fire. An alarm was raised, but owing to the early hour, the flame, aided by a high wind, had made rapid progress before assistance could be procured. Two policemen - P.C.'s Lobeley and Brown were first on the scene, attracted by the huge glare in the sky, visible for miles around. The Fire Brigade was called, but it took almost an hour for the first engine to reach the scene, by which time the fire had become general and the whole buildings were in danger.

The larger engine was planted in Messrs Fisher's quarry, being the nearest point to the water. It had scarcely got to work when the hose burst and was rendered useless.

The Mustard Mill of Mr. Barringer and the houses adjoining were at this time in great danger, the whole being surrounded by dry stacks of timber, upon which sparks were continually falling. The engine was at length brought to the spot and a line of men was formed to the stream. Buckets were plentiful and assistance prompt. The firemen now displayed considerable energy and those buildings were soon out of danger. The Wood Shop, Engine House and chief factory, in fact all of the buildings connected with the Wood Yard, were one mass of smouldering ruins.

The whole of the made up stock, except what had been saved by individual assistance was destroyed, but the Wood Yard, which contains a large amount of valuable timber, was preserved.

It is at present impossible to say how the fire originated, but we understand the greater part destroyed was insured.

Appendix 1

HISTORY OF 'THE LOOKING GLASS BOX'

In the search for attractive novelties for Christmas biscuit boxes, someone suggested that a box decorated with Tenniel's illustrations of 'Alice's Adventures in Wonderland,' or 'Through The Looking Glass,' might prove popular. It was decided that Lewis Carroll should be approached and Miss Mary E. Manners, who had entertained him on two or three occasions, was asked to write to him with a view to obtaining his permission for this use of illustrations. His reply is as follows :

Ch. Ch. Oxford
April 14th 1891

Dear Miss Manners,

I fear I must trouble you for more information before I can answer your letter, as I do not in the least know what a 'children's tin' is. The biscuit boxes I buy are covered with paper, which of course might be decorated with pictures : but I think it would be degrading Art to do so, as they would necessarily be torn to pieces when opening the box.

Mansfield is not in my line of travel I fear, but I will remember about the Works there if ever I find myself near it.

Ch. Ch. Oxford
April 21st 1891

Dear Miss Manners

I have received, inspected and returned to Messrs. Barringer and Co. a number of pieces of tin and two little boxes, decorated with pictures which are evidently of a permanent character and (so far as I can judge) of considerable artistic merit : so I am happy to give my permission for the 'Alice' pictures to be similarly treated.

The question remains, 'what are nursery tins?' (To my dull mind) as far off solution as ever. Were I a child and had one of these boxes before me, my chief anxiety would be to get an answer to the question 'what is it for?' You will guess from this how very limited an acquaintance I have with nurseries and nursery children.

Appendix 2 (Page 1)

P.S. One possible 'nursery' use for such a box occurs to me. It might hold flour or starch, or whatever it is that is dredged over babies after they have been washed and is, no doubt, the cause of their continual crying. I should wail, most of the day, if so treated. Is that the 'raison d'etre' of nursery tins?

Ch. Ch. Oxford
February 14th 1892

Dear Miss Manners,

I should like very much to see the proofs, on tin, of the 'Alice' pictures (and not the coloured sketches), but I need not wait for that to say that your brother is quite welcome to put 'by permission of Lewis Carroll,' or 'of the author,' whichever he prefers.

Ch. Ch. Oxford
April 1st 1982

Dear Miss Manners,

The 'Alice' tin is indeed a great success. Is it possible to multiply it to any extent in duplicate? I've not the least idea how such a thing could be done, they look as if painted by hand.

The box you sent was not sufficiently packed for a journey. It had received several bruises and indentations, in spite of the paste board. If ever I get your brother to take an order for a number of them, and to send them to my little friends, I should wish them to be packed in wooden boxes, (for which I would pay; they might be quite rough, like packing cases and with lids nailed on, not hinged). Before making up a list I would be glad to know, (1) wether there is any choice of different size and shapes of boxes, or if they would all be duplicates of the one sent to me, (2) What would be the cost of say 50 of them, packing included?

There are many letters from Lewis Carroll in existence showing his great interest in the production of the box and his expressions of satisfaction as to the way the work was carried out.

Appendix 2 (Page 2)

7 Lushington Road

Eastbourne

August 29th 1892

Dear Mr. Manners,

The two boxes arrived safe and have given great pleasure to the two little friends to whom I sent them, viz. The 2 children of the Duchess of Albany : and, as they are sure to show them to their friends, it will be a fairly good advertisement of this article

One difficulty I have felt as to accepting your offer was, that you offered 50 and I have at least 100 young friends to whom I should like to send them. However, I am not above accepting presents and, after what you say, I will gladly accept these.

I will send a full list directly. Today I can only give a few names.:

1 box - The Misses Dodgson

The Chestnuts

Guildford.

2 boxes - Misses B & G Dodgson

The Court

Cleobury North

Bridgnorth

Ch. Ch. Oxford

October 13th 1892

Dear Mr. Manners,

I feel impelled, in sending you so long a list of Oxford friends, to whom I wish to present your charming biscuit boxes, to represent to you that even the most lavish generosity may reasonably be expected to have some limit - I have just made out a list of of all the friends whom I wish thus to gratify - and the number is 364! You have already most kindly given me about 150. Suppose we consider those to be presented and let me pay for the other 200.

Believe me,

Very truly yours,

C.L.Dodgson

Appendix 2 (Page 3)

Many eminent names appear in the list of his friends to whom he wished boxes to be sent. The following is a selection of them :

J.Tenniel (later Sir John Tenniel), illustrator of his books.

Mrs.Ritchie (Miss Alice Liddell), for whom the stories were written and who later sold, in 1928, the original manuscript of *Alice in Wonderland.*

Miss C.Rossetti

Miss M.Terry

Miss V.Beerbohm Tree

Miss Isa Bowman

Miss Nellie Bowman

Miss Maggie Bowman

Miss Empsie Bowman

(The author took a great personal interest in the Bowman children - later they became professional actresses).

Mrs. DuMaurier

Ch. Ch. Oxford

December 1st 1892

Dear Mr. Manners,

    I am dismayed to hear the 'Looking Glass' boxes are to have so short an existence. I had fancied they would be popular and would go on selling for years to come. The '110' I named, brought me to the end of my list, but I should certainly like my friends to have another chance of buying a few. Would you kindly put aside another 50? I should be much more comfortable about it if you would get those biscuit people to agree to your selling me the empty boxes. I must have had and bespoken from £8 to £10 worth.

    My friends are pretty sure to want them empty. They are not at all likely to care to desert Huntley and Palmer and buy biscuits from Ireland.

    You say, 'I had hoped to have had the privilege of producing an 'Alice in Wonderland' box. Does that mean that you have abandoned the idea?

Very truly yours

C.L.Dodgson

Appendix 2 (Page 4)

Invitation to the Foundation Stone Laying of the Works extension, Rock Valley in 1919.

Invitation to the Annual Dinner of Barringer Wallace and Manners employees in 1899.

Appendix 3

PROGRAMME

VISIT OF

THEIR MAJESTIES

KING GEORGE V.

AND

QUEEN MARY

TO

NOTTS. AND DERBYSHIRE

JUNE 25TH, 1914

Programme for the visit of their majesties King George V and Queen Mary in 1914 - title page.

Appendix 4 (Page 1)

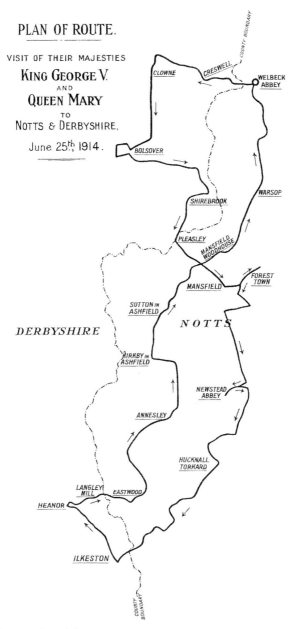

PLAN OF ROUTE.

VISIT OF THEIR MAJESTIES
KING GEORGE V.
AND
QUEEN MARY
TO
NOTTS & DERBYSHIRE,

June 25th, 1914.

CLOWNE

CRESWELL

WELBECK ABBEY

BOLSOVER

WARSOP

SHIREBROOK

PLEASLEY

MANSFIELD WOODHOUSE

MANSFIELD

FOREST TOWN

SUTTON IN ASHFIELD

NOTTS

DERBYSHIRE

KIRKBY IN ASHFIELD

NEWSTEAD ABBEY

ANNESLEY

HUCKNALL TORKARD

LANGLEY MILL

EASTWOOD

HEANOR

ILKESTON

COUNTY BOUNDARY

Plan of route for visit

Appendix 4 (Page 2)

PROGRAMME.

	Arrive. a.m.	Depart. p.m.
MANSFIELD - - - - - - -	11.52	—

Presentations on Stand in the Market Place :

The DUKE OF PORTLAND will present

The Mayor of Mansfield (Alderman T. TAYLOR).

SIR ARTHUR B. MARKHAM, Bt., M.P.

The MAYOR will present

The Mayoress (Miss TAYLOR).

Miss CONSTANCE LEILA TAYLOR, aged 9, granddaughter of the Mayor, will present a Bouquet to HER MAJESTY THE QUEEN.

The Town Clerk (Mr. HARROP WHITE).
Councillor HOUFTON, Deputy Mayor.
The Mayor's Chaplain (The Rev. W. LILLEY).
Alderman CRAMPTON.
Alderman MALTBY.
Alderman ALCOCK.
Alderman SINGLETON.
Alderman WILSON.
Councillor HALL.
Councillor COLLINS.
Councillor T. SMITH.

The DUKE OF PORTLAND will present

Mr. H. E. HOLLINS
(Chairman of the Hospital Board).

Programme for visit - itinerary for Mansfield - Page 1

Appendix 4 (Page 3)

PROGRAMME.

———

	Arrive. p.m.	Depart. p.m.
After the Presentations HIS MAJESTY, by pressing an Electric Button, will open the King Edward Memorial Wing of the Mansfield Hospital -	—	12. 2
Visit Messrs. BARRINGER, WALLIS AND MANNERS' Works (20 minutes) - -	12. 7	12.27

Presentations :

Mr. W. H. REDDAN (Director)
and Mrs. REDDAN.

Mr. I. H. WALLIS (Director)
and Mrs. WALLIS.

Mr. G. N. F. REDDAN (Director)
and Mrs. REDDAN.

Mr. R. MANNERS (Director).

	Arrive.	Depart.
Visit Crown Farm Colliery Village, Forest Town - - - - -	12.42	12.52

Presentations at the Institute :

Directors of the Bolsover Colliery
Company :

Mr. R. M. KNOWLES, Chairman
of Directors.

Mr. J. P. HOUFTON, Managing
Director.

Mr. W. H. CARTER, Manager of
Colliery.

Notts. Miners' Association Representatives :

Mr. J. G. HANCOCK, M.P., Agent.

Mr. C. BUNFIELD, Secretary.

Mr. W. CARTER, Assistant Secretary.

Mr. L. SPENCER, Treasurer.

Programme for visit - itinerary - Page 2

Appendix 4 (Page 4)

THE ROYAL VISIT TO NOTTS. AND DERBYSHIRE

LETTER FROM THE KING

The Duke of Portland K.G. has received the following letter from the King :

Buckingham Palace
27th June 1914

My dear Portland,

It was a great satisfaction to the Queen and me to carry out, during our stay at Welbeck, the three days tour arranged by you in parts of Nottinghamshire and Derbyshire.

I would ask you to convey to the Mayors and Local Authorities respectively my appreciation of the admirable arrangements made by them for our reception.

We were much impressed by the enthusiastic welcome given to us in the many boroughs and local centres through which we passed, by the vast gatherings of school children, and by the fact that so many of the inhabitants had decorated their own houses, and we warmly acknowledge these proofs of loyalty and affection.

The visit to Messrs. Barringer's Works at Mansfield and to the Crown Farm Colliery village, Forest Town, were incidents of especial interest to us, and we enjoyed the opportunities of seeing something of the natural beauties of the country through which we passed.

I was glad to notice the strong muster of Territorials in the different towns, and to see so many naval and military veterans, while the big parades of the various boys' organisations testified to the popularity of these movements.

The police arrangements in the boroughs and throughout our long motor journeys were most efficiently planned and carried out, and I congratulate the Chief Constables upon the successful results of their careful and well thought out plans.

In conclusion, I thank you most sincerely for all the trouble you have bestowed upon the preparations for our visit, of which the Queen and I will always preserve the happiest recollections.

Believe me, very sincerely yours,
(Signed) George R.I.

Appendix 4 (Page 5)

BUCKINGHAM PALACE

4th July 1914.

Dear Sir,

I am commanded by the Queen to convey to you an expression of Her Majesty's sincere thanks for the case containing a number of articles manufactured by your Firm, which you have been good enough to send for the Queen's acceptance.

Her Majesty much appreciates the kind thought which has prompted you to send these articles, and is greatly pleased to possess them as a pleasing souvenir of her visit to your Works.

I am,

Yours faithfully,

E. W. Wallington

Private Secretary.

W.H.REDDAN ESQ,
    Managing Director,
        Messrs Barringer Wallis & Manners Ltd.
        MANSFIELD.

Appendix 4 (Page 6)

Poster for St. Dunstan's Hostel and Concert at Arcadia Hall, 1918

Appendix 5

Extensions to the factories of BARRINGER WALLIS & MANNERS, Ltd. MANSFIELD

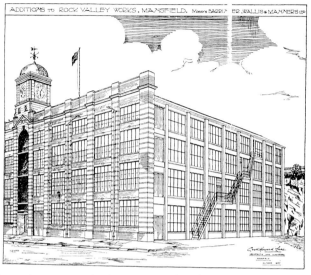

There has recently been completed an industrial building which represents a very successful attempt to achieve the modern ideals of economy without sacrifice to cheapness. This building was erected for Barringer Wallis and Manners Ltd. of Mansfield as an extension to their tin-box making factory and it exhibits all the characteristics of good solid British building tradition.

The site of the building is in an old quarry and at the rear the ground level is at about third floor level. This quarry has been practically filled in with waste stone and earth which has become fairly well consolidated.

Before construction could be started some cottages had to be demolished and the face of the quarry required trimming in parts where it was overhanging. The work of clearing the site, which also involved removing filling about fifteen feet deep, was commenced on August 14th 1926 and was completed by the end of September. Excavation for the foundations was completed about the same time. The building was completed and handed to the owners on June 1st 1927

(Extracts from a Mansfield Reporter article, November 11th 1927)

Appendix 6

BY APPOINTMENT

BARRINGER WALLIS & MANNERS LTD.
MANSFIELD
ENGLAND

BRANCH
OFFICES
LONDON
LIVERPOOL
GLASGOW

Makers of

DECORATED TIN BOXES
METAL ADVERTISEMENTS

TELEPHONE
MANSFIELD
1144
TELEGRAMS
DECBOX
MANSFIELD

July 1939.

Dear Sirs,

After giving very careful consideration and much deliberation to the matter, we have completed arrangements to associate ourselves with The Metal Box Company Limited, and thus, whilst maintaining our own organisation, to have the benefit of their resources.

We have given much thought to this and other aspects which may have a bearing upon the service we have always offered to our customers, and have decided to take this step which we believe is best calculated to maintain and strengthen the position.

The personnel and management of our Company and its policy will continue unchanged. You may rely, therefore, upon a continuance of the same service, quality and price basis as before, together with such advantages as the association of interests, technical knowledge, and the pooling of resources may provide.

Enquiries should, of course, be sent direct to us or to our representatives, as in the past, but in addition, if communicated to any branch of The Metal Box Company Limited, will be forwarded to us.

We take this opportunity of thanking you for the business you have entrusted to us in the past, and hope that you will continue to give us your confidence.

Yours faithfully,

BARRINGER, WALLIS & MANNERS LTD.,

JOINT MANAGING DIRECTOR.

Appendix 7

BARRINGER WALLIS AND MANNERS
SOME NOTABLE DATES

1839 - David Cooper Barringer took over the mustard business of John Ellis.

1861 - The death occurred of David Cooper Barringer.

1862 - The late David Cooper Barringer's mustard business in Rock Valley was assigned to his brother, Robert Barringer, who came from Wakefield and formed a partnership with Edwin Brown, also of Wakefield. The firm became known as Barringer and Brown.

1879 - Isaac Henry Wallis came to Mansfield to become a partner in Barringer and Brown.

1880 - Walter Barringer, son of Robert Barringer, became a partner of Barringer and Brown.

1890 - Robert Barringer retired. Two companies were formed: Barringer and Company, mustard manufacturers and Barringer Wallis and Manners, tinplate decorators and printers.

1895 - Barringer Wallis and Manners became a limited liability company.

1897 - Expansion to Sutton-in-Ashfield. Oddicroft Mill purchased, plus 10 acres of land for £2,800.

1900 - (1 January) To celebrate the turn of the century Queen Victoria arranged for some tin boxes containing chocolates to be sent to the British troops fighting in Africa in the Boer War. The chocolates were manufactured by Rowntrees of York, the tin boxes by Barringer Wallis and Manners.

1902 - (5 March) The death occurred of William Reddan aged 67. He had been the firm's senior sales representative and had worked for Barringer Wallis and Manners for 40 years. 'No firm ever had a more faithful, more diligent, or more cheerful representative.' Such was the tribute paid by the company at the time of his death.

1905 - (26 June) The death occurred of Charles Manners of 'Edenbank,' Crow Hill Drive, Mansfield, the founder of Barringer Wallis and Manners. He was the husband of Emily Barringer, the daughter of Robert Barringer.

Appendix 8 (Page 1)

1905 - (8 November) The death occurred of Robert Barringer. A native of Church Brampton, Northamptonshire, he had married Anne Maria Wallis.

1909 - (30 July) The official opening of the new building, including the canteen, (Arcadia Hall).

1912 - (13 February) The death occurred of Walter Barringer of 'Innisdoon,' Crow Hill Drive, Mansfield. He was Chairman of the Directors of Barringer and Co. a director of Barringer Wallis and Manners and also the Mansfield Sand Co.

1914 - (25 June) King George V and Queen Mary visited Mansfield and district, which included a tour of the Rock Valley Works.

1919 - (6 June) Foundation stone for Tower Block laid by William Holmes Reddan at the Rock Valley Works.

1923 - (7 February) The death occurred of William Holmes Reddan, the Managing Director of Barringer Wallis and Manners. Robert Manners and Gustave Reddan were appointed Joint Managing Directors.

1927 - (1 June) Further extensions to the Rock Valley Works, (Clock Tower and Tower Block extension) completed.

1933 - The death occurred of Isaac Henry Wallis. He was Chairman of Directors of Barringer Wallis and Manners.

1939 - Barringer Wallis and Manners merged their interests with the Metal Box Company.

1944 - (16 January) The death occurred of Robert Manners, aged 55, of New Farm, Blidworth.

1947 - (31 March) Gustave Reddan and William Graham Maltby, an ex-director of Barringer Wallis and Manners, retired.

1950 - The death occurred of Gustave Nathanial Reddan.

1953 - The death occurred of William Graham Maltby.

Appendix 8 (Page 2)

JOYCE BRYAN'S WARTIME MEMORIES OF THE METAL BOX COMPANY (FORMERLY BARRINGER WALLIS AND MANNERS)

(Reproduced by kind permission of the Old Mansfield Society from their publication *Mansfield in World War II*)

I joined the company in 1942 as a teenager doing respirators for gas masks... also mess tins ... and bomb tails. It was shift work, but I was unable to go on nights because I wasn't old enough. You had to be eighteen to go on nights. So, that put me out of nights. I just did days and afternoons. The morning shift was six am till two pm and the afternoon shift was two till ten pm. Hand presses were used at this time. Power presses came later on. Passes were needed to enter the works gates and you had to carry your gas mask with you for which the firm provided a carrying tin. In addition to the gas masks and mess tins in the early period of the war they were also contracted to make the Boyes Anti-tank Rifle, a one-man weapon which fired an armour-piercing half-inch round shell. During the invasion scares of 1940 and 1941 they were standard issue for units on anti-invasion duties and for the RAF Regiment. Later on the company made the Very pistol and the Sten machine carbine.

Another aspect of the war effort was the raising of money for War Bonds. The schemes were to raise £5000, the notional cost of a Spitfire aircraft. The Metal Box group set up one of these schemes and all member companies of the group participated. By May 1941 an aircraft had been bought - Spitfire Mk2b, serial P8389, carrying the name 'Metabox'. It survived the war, being scrapped in 1947.

Appendix 9